Praises for the book…

"Whether you know it or not, we all have blind spots. In his book, BlindSpots: Why Good People Make Bad Choices, Kevin reveals his real-life and riveting story about his blind spots that lead him down a frightening path he had never anticipated. His journey is gripping, powerful and thought-provoking. You will find this book insightful and a page-turner…a read that you won't want to put down until the end. Kevin is scheduled to speak at our annual conference and I can't wait to hear his story in person!"

> - Nancy Waterhouse
> Executive Director, Ohio Government Finance Officers Association

"A great book for business professionals and all walks of life! Blind Spots is an introspective journey into one's past and discovering your true drivers and motivations in life. Only by understanding our past can we make better decisions that will shape our future."

> - Sean Nakamura
> President 2016-18, AGA Hawaii Chapter

"Great book for anyone in any walk of life! Any individual can relate to the story told by Kevin in this book. We all find ourselves faced with difficult, and not so difficult, decisions but don't really think about, or allow ourselves to think about, whether we are making those decisions with open minds or ones clouded by the BLIND SPOTS as pointed out by Kevin."

> - Torpey White
> CPA, CITP, CISA, CGEIT, CGMA

"The detail and approach to sharing your story kept me on the edge of my seat and wanting to keep reading more! Well done. I felt like I was living the experience with you."

> - John P. Waters
> CEO, Waters Business Consulting Group, LLC

"Read this book! Kevin is a masterful storyteller. His willingness to be vulnerable and transparent is admirable and draws you right into the story. The lessons he learned and now shares in his book are powerfully thought-provoking. This is a home-run!"

> -Tom Griffith
> Founder, Making Better Happen, LLC.

"The book shared many lessons about the various 'Blind Spots' we all face. I took the opportunity to reflect on each one to see if I had the potential to get caught up in my own 'stuff'. It was a great read all the way through. Not only is the story captivating, but the real-life lessons that Kevin shares are easily adaptable to any situation. I highly recommend this book. And, as someone who has hired Kevin to speak to my organization, he is an amazing speaker as well. Let him bring his insights to your organization. You'll be glad you did."

- Lisa Ryan
Founder | Chief Appreciation Strategist, Grategy, LLC.

"Every leader has blind spots. The biggest challenge is discovering them before it's too late. Kevin McCarthy masterfully draws us into his incredible leadership journey while exposing us to the blind spots that can cause good leaders to make bad choices. Every leader should read this book!"

-Heather Christie
CEO, Evolve Global

"When I started reading this book, it was hard for me to put down! It held my attention & I couldn't wait to get back to reading it. Kevin McCarthy has captured the reasons we sometimes make bad decisions. Blind Spots is truly an insightful, self-improvement & suspenseful book."

- Brenda Collins Johnson
OEA Coordinator & Business Teacher, retired

"This book is like no other out there. It's so captivating I could not put the book down once I started reading. It is a powerful lesson to all of us what Blind Spots we all have and how to be aware of them…Kevin bares his soul and shares with complete transparency in order to help others!... Riveting story about truth, even though sometimes you feel like you are reading fiction, it's that great!

- Todd Powell
General Sales Manager, Wilson Ford

Kevin McCarthy

BLINDSPOTS

WHY GOOD PEOPLE MAKE BAD CHOICES

KEVIN MCCARTHY

Healy Quinn Publishers
West Linn

HEALY QUINN
PUBLISHERS

This book is based on the true-life experiences, perspectives and recollec-
tions of the author. Much care has been given to ensure the facts and details
included are as accurate as possible. To protect the rights of those involved
or whose paths have crossed the author's, some of the names have been
changed. All the names of the co-defendants in the case, with the exception
of the CEO, have been changed to allow them to rebuild their lives and tell
their own stories, if and when they feel ready.
I wish them all the very best!

For speaking engagements please contact Speaking@KevinMcCarthy.com,
or visit www.KevinMcCarthy.com.

For order or bulk purchases of this book, please write
Books@KevinMcCarthy.com.

Library of Congress Control Number: 2017909411
Healy Quinn Publishers, West Linn, Oregon

Edited by Heather Rose Walters
Cover design by Kerry Ellis

McCarthy, Kevin
    Blindspots: Why good people make bad choices / Kevin McCarthy

ISBN: 0-9991034-2-3
ISBN-13: 978-0-9991034-2-5

Printed in the United States of America

DEDICATION

This book is dedicated to my best friend, soul mate, and wife for more than thirty years, Rachel. Your enduring spirit, consistent faith, and undying commitment to me and our marriage continues to have me in awe. I don't think I could have walked through this experience without you walking with me.
I am a better man because of you.

I also dedicate this book to our two amazing children, Christopher and Noelle, who persevered through the absence of their father during critical stages of their own development as young people. You have both made good decisions that are yielding good fruit in your lives. I am incredibly proud of you both!

To my parents, Jim and Judi, and to Rachel's parents, Ray and Katy, who sacrificed so much to walk with us through this incredibly challenging journey. And, to my sisters, Tracy and Heather who continue to demonstrate their unconditional love and support. Thank you. I love and appreciate you all.

I am truly blessed to have such an amazing family.

Finally, thank you to the many friends, colleagues and clients who reviewed the book before its release and provided final feedback, reviews and corrections. I appreciate you all!

BLINDSPOTS

WHY GOOD PEOPLE MAKE BAD CHOICES

CONTENTS

CHAPTER ONE:

BLIND SPOTS DISCOVERED

MY ATTORNEY'S OFFICE

Carol, my attorney, escorted me through a long hallway, past several private offices, cubicles, and conference rooms in the Seattle Federal Public Defenders building. I was dreading this meeting, just as I'd dreaded our previous six. The government had seized all of our assets, so I was stuck with this assigned Public Defender. It seemed like she would do anything to get me off her caseload – she didn't want to fight for me, she just wanted me to sign a plea bargain. She wanted me to agree to serve up to 10 years in a federal prison for a crime I didn't *knowingly* commit.

We didn't even make it to our seats before the argument began.

"Have you decided to sign the plea bargain?" Carol said matter-of-factly.

"Carol, I am not signing any plea bargain!" I exclaimed. "I did not know my boss was committing a crime. I've watched enough Law and Order to know that one has to have intent to commit fraud!"

"Kevin, we've been around this…" Carol started to point something out, but then stopped mid-sentence. "Wait a minute. I just realized why you and I are not seeing eye-to-eye. You're seeing this through a moral perspective. I'm seeing it through a *legal* perspective." She sat back with a look of both puzzlement and satisfaction.

I was perplexed. Though I didn't yet fully grasp her comment, I had this strange sense of peace. I felt, for the first time, that we were actually making progress.

"Kevin," she went on, "I totally believe you that you didn't know your boss was committing a crime. In fact, I'm confident that I can convince a jury that you didn't know. But that will not matter in a courtroom. The judge will simply turn to the jury and issue instructions that sound like this…"

Mimicking the judge, Carol continued in a stern, judicial tone, "Ladies and gentlemen of the jury. It does not matter what you think about Kevin's knowledge of the crime. He is not being charged with fraud. He is being charged with *conspiracy* to commit fraud. Under the Federal statutes, only one person in a conspiracy needs to know a crime is being committed. Therefore, your job today is simply to decide if Kevin's actions aided his boss in the crime."

Carol then continued with a softer, more compassionate tone. "So, you see, Kevin, the minute you placed the envelopes in the mail at your boss' request, you became a co-conspirator in his mail fraud."

All I could do was sit back and ponder her comments. This was the first time I was confronted with the concept that two people can experience the same event, while having two completely different perspectives. This is when I first became aware of the concept of blind spots.

I finally understood profoundly that you do not know what you do not know. I had experienced a phenomenon: that the reality you believe you have experienced can actually be flawed and inaccurate.

Carol and I reviewed the plea bargain together. I was finally ready to sign it.

Carol refers to me as "an unwitting accomplice" in my boss' stock fraud. Over seven years, Lawrence took more than $91 million from over 5,000 investors in what the FBI called the largest stock fraud in the history of the state of Washington.

Out of thirty-four employees, twelve men, including Lawrence, would eventually spend time in a federal prison for their actions. I believe only three of the twelve actually knew they were involved, and willingly participated in Lawrence's scheme. The rest of us didn't know. But, from an outsiders' perspective, it would be natural to think, "You *should* have known." Therein lies the problem with blind spots.

By signing the plea bargain, I agreed to serve up to ten years. I was later sentenced to 48 months as a result of my co-operation. Due to the prison's good behavior policy, and voluntarily attending a 500-hour Cognitive Behavioral Psychology program offered in the prison, I only had to serve 33 months.

Blind spots are those hidden biases, implicit associations, memory traps and thinking errors that affect your behavior and decision-making.

We don't know what we don't know. Of course, this is the nature of blind spots. We all deal with blind spots at different levels, and in different times or situations.

Becoming aware of the idea that you have blind spots is the first step to mitigating their effects. This stage of unawareness is called the Blindspot Blindspot. That is, you tend to think you are above average, are in full control of your mental faculties, and that you make good, unbiased decisions -- at least most of the time. You want to feel you are doing well and "have your stuff together." Welcome to the Blind Spot Zone!

To give you a better understanding of where my mind was

at during this ordeal, you need to understand some highlights from my entrepreneurial past. My personal life and upbringing, my professional experience, my role models, and of course, Hollywood, all played a significant role in framing my reality in such a way that would allow me to behave contrary to my moral compass. This mental framework is my worldview.

Blind Spot Challenge: What are your blind spots doing to you?

WORLDVIEW

WHAT WAS I THINKING?

We all have a worldview. Most of us, however, do not think too much about it.

Your worldview is a work-in-progress. It is constantly being updated and altered based on the events in your life; it's molded and fortified based on the tragedies you've endured, the positive and negative experiences you've had, and the disappointments you've faced. It is shaped by how you were raised, by the socio-economic environment in which you grew up, and the circumstances in which you now find yourself. Your perception of reality is influenced by the input you allow to infiltrate your mind: the media, your education, and the opinions of others. Your worldview most often operates on autopilot in the background of your mind, at the subconscious level.

Simply put, your **worldview** is your mental framework of reality. It is your personal belief system about all the things in life.

German philosopher Immanuel Kant first coined the term "worldview" by combining two German words: *Welt*, meaning "world" and *Anschauung* meaning "Conception, idea, opinion or view."

Blind spots reside within your worldview and warp your perceptions of reality. They allow good people to make bad choices; choices that you might not otherwise make if your perceptions were more accurate.

For example, on November 17, 1973 President Richard Nixon uttered the now infamous words, "I am not a crook," as he denied his involvement in the Watergate break-in. Even after the unequivocal proof of his involvement in the crimes came to light, "Nixon himself never admitted to any criminal wrongdoing, though he did acknowledge using poor judgment."[1] Poor judgment, or a blind spot?

Did Nixon really believe he was innocent? That he merely used poor judgment? It's easy for us to judge his actions and the results. It's *not* so easy to determine what he truly believed. We can agree, though, that he definitely used poor judgment.

You've seen the television crime dramas: police officers march into the precinct with a prisoner in handcuffs who proclaims, "I'm innocent, I tell ya!" The officers barely bat an eye. More often than not, they jokingly respond, "Yeah, yeah, heard it all before, pal!"

This was my mindset until that dreadfully wonderful day in Carol's office when my blind spots first became clear. My worldview had allowed me to believe that the decisions I made to follow my boss' orders were "good," even though, in hindsight, there should have been plenty of red flags and warning signs telling me to run from the situation. In fact, the Federal Prosecutor said that, had I resigned about halfway through my tenure, I would never have been in trouble. *Now he tells me!*

---

[1] Retrieved from http://www.history.com/topics/watergate

Despite the obvious red flags, I had no idea, within the context of my worldview, that my boss was selling stock illegally. I had no idea he had no intention of ever launching a publicly held company.

"I was innocent, I tell ya!"

But I wasn't!

CHAPTER TWO:

THE BACKSTORY

You better believe that right now, blind spots exist in your worldview. No one is immune. The only way to fully understand where blind spots hide, and how to mitigate their impact is to, 1) Review your past; 2) Evaluate your present; and 3) Have a clear vision for your future.

With that in mind, the next few chapters will paint a quick picture of my journey, and the blind spots that led up to working for Lawrence.

DRIVEN TO BE WEALTHY

While in prison, I enjoyed frequent visits from my wife, Rachel. She would visit monthly, bringing our two children every other month. Christopher was thirteen when I started my sentence, and Noelle was eleven. My parents lived out of state, but came as often as they could. Other friends would drop in occasionally.

The visiting room resembled a hospital cafeteria: nothing on the walls, and thirty round tables scattered around, with four to five chairs each. Visitors checked in with the guard who sat in front of a computer next to the entrance. He always acted busy after checking everyone in. We all assumed he was playing Solitaire.

Once the visitor's identity was confirmed and verified on the authorized visitor list, they were allowed to enter the room unescorted.

Inmates were allowed to greet their visitors with a quick

hug and kiss. Rachel and I always pushed that to the limit, until we heard the guard clearing his throat with a friendly warning.

We would then proceed to our table of choice. Visitors could stay for the entire length of visiting hours, from 8:30 am to 3:30 pm, if they desired, during which handholding and putting our arms around each other was allowed. No kissing or anything more affectionate than a side-hug was permitted as we continued.

There were soda and snack machines where the visitor could purchase items for the visit. Inmates could share, and that was always a treat, but we could never bring anything back into the compound.

During one of these visits with my parents, who were also investors in the company, we were reminiscing about how we all thought we were going to sell our stock and become wealthy. This must be what prompted my mother to say, "You probably don't remember this, Kevin, but, when you were little, you used to say, 'Mom and Dad, someday I am going to be a multimillionaire and buy you that motor home you always dream of.'"

Apparently becoming wealthy was on my mind at an early age.

FOR THE LOVE OF MONEY

There is nothing inherently wrong with prosperity or wealth. Money itself is amoral; it is neither good nor evil. There is an ancient saying that often gets twisted. Often, people will say, "money is the root of all evil." Sorry, folks, but Jesus never said that. The actual text, Timothy 16:10, says "For the *love* of money is the root of all evil."

When you are so in love with money, and what money can

buy, that your pursuits become obsessive, blind spots spring up. Your reality can easily become skewed.

Mine did.

I suffered from the Generosity Blind Spot. But wait! How can generosity be a blind spot?

GENEROSITY BLIND SPOT

I used to think of myself as a generous person; I donated regularly and generously to a multitude of non-profits. What I didn't realize is that I was *also* simultaneously greedy. Yes, greed and generosity co-exist, and do more often than you'd think.

My generosity, though genuine, was also a perfect cover-up for my greed. I could justify my lust for wealth by explaining how much my money was helping others. It did, but it masked a subtle, unconscious character defect: greed.

It's easier to see the blind spots in others than it is to see them in yourself. This was no different for my Generosity Blind Spot when I was working for Lawrence.

I was the manager of the Investor Relations department (a.k.a. "IR"). My primary role was to clean up a very messy database which contained potentially erroneous stockholder information. Lawrence suspected that the previous person issued shares of stock to people who had not actually paid for them. He was right. The data was a mess. My staff and I had to do some forensic work to decipher the real investments from the many unauthorized gifts.

The team was also tasked with keeping the investors informed of any news that Lawrence wanted them to know about the "imminent" IPO; we monitored the rumor mill. I spoke with a pantheon of investors every week.

Like my own original investment, many of the investors used their last $5,000 or $10,000 to buy stock with the hopes of a quick and lucrative return.

> *Action tip: If you ever have the opportunity to invest in anything that offers "quick" and "lucrative" returns, run fast and far.*

The stock was selling for $1 per share, with the promise of a four-to-one split before the IPO. In other words, for every dollar you invested, you would end up with four shares of stock. Then the public offering was expected to open on the NASDAQ between $18 and $20 per share. If you do the math, a $10,000 investment would be worth between $720,000 and $880,000 on opening day.

Yes, in hindsight I feel ridiculous that I fell for this scam.

OMG! HE ACTUALLY FELL FOR IT!

Which reminds me, in 2016 I presented the opening keynote speech for a Fraud Awareness conference in the Bahamas. There were a number of government officials in the audience, including the Senior Investigator for the Securities Commission of the Bahamas, the equivalent of the United States Securities and Exchange Commission (SEC). My client introduced me to him just before the speech.

That was awkward.

Afterward, I decided to strike up a conversation with this officer. To my knowledge I had not yet had anyone with his title in one of my audiences. I'll call him Edward.

"Edward, thank you for listening to my presentation. May I ask you a question?" I was completely intrigued at how his highly suspicious mind might respond.

"Sure." His one-word reply had almost no emotion. Dead-pan.

I continued with a bit of trepidation: "I'm just curious... what went through your mind, from the time you arrived this morning to the end of my presentation?"

He chuckled, his first sign of warmth, as he thought back through his reactions.

He explained in a concise, chronological sequence:

"I don't believe this guy."
"Oh no, this guy didn't really fall for that, did he?"
"OMG! He did! He actually fell for it!"
"I enjoyed your presentation," he finished with a smile.

We then continued a very warm conversation. He gave me his card. His associate recommended that I facilitate my full-day *Beyond the Blind Spot Zone* training program to their entire Securities Commission workgroup. Oh, the irony!

MASKING THE GREED

Working with Lawrence, I heard countless stories from investors who all expected a huge windfall, about the many good things they planned to do with their money. They would build new libraries, orphanages, feed the hungry -- the list goes on. Many were victims of the Generosity Blind Spot. Most, if not all of these people, were good at heart. Unfortunately, just like me, their Generosity Blind Spot got in their way.

Good people make bad choices when you rationalize your

greed by talking about all the good things you will do with the money you obtain, all the while knowing, deep down, you mostly just want to spend it on your own material happiness.

You don't like feeling greedy, so you try to reduce your discomfort by telling others (and yourself) that you're going to do good things with your wealth.

Yeah, sure you are.

This mental conflict is what psychologists call, Cognitive Dissonance.

DISSONANCE THEORY

Cognitive Dissonance refers to conflicting attitudes, beliefs or behaviors in one person. This produces a feeling of discomfort, which leads to an alteration in one of those attitudes, beliefs or behaviors, to reduce the discomfort and restore balance.

For example, many people smoke (behavior), even though they know that smoking causes cancer (cognition). Usually, to reduce their discomfort, they develop the attitude that they "don't care", or in some cases, they don't believe the evidence. They alter their belief.

> *Blind Spot Challenge: Stress can be caused by doing the things you know you shouldn't, or not doing the things you know you should. What is causing your stress?*

"Festinger's (1957) cognitive dissonance theory suggests that we have an inner drive to hold *all* our attitudes and beliefs in harmony, and avoid disharmony (or dissonance).[2]"

Most of the more than 5,000 investors did not come from a place of wealth. They were ordinary, middle-class citizens who invested a significant portion of their small net worth. Some even *borrowed* money to make the investment.

Dreaming of lifestyles to which they were unaccustomed, and buying things they desired, but normally wouldn't buy, created dissonance. Talking about spending the money on others, or on charitable causes, reduced the dissonance. And it created a blind spot.

MATERIALISM BLIND SPOT

The Materialism Blind Spot causes good people to make bad choices when they mitigate their dissonance. This blind spot almost single-handedly drives the success of the lottery system. With no other practical means of attaining wealth, you dream of winning the lottery. The same thing happens when entrepreneurs dream of reaching some pinnacle of success. You believe that money will solve all your problems and make life much easier. Though there might be some truth to that, the attainment of wealth can often actually have an adverse effect on the way many of you think and act. In essence, you can become a very different person – usually not for the better.

"Indeed, the Certified Financial Planner Board of Standards says nearly a third of lottery winners declare bankruptcy—meaning they were *worse* off than before. Other studies show that lottery winners frequently become estranged from family and friends, and incur a greater incidence of depression, drug

---

[2] McLeod, Saul, *Cognitive Dissonance* (2008, updated 2014). Retrieved from http://www.simplypsychology.org/cognitive-dissonance.html

and alcohol abuse, divorce, and suicide than the average American.

No wonder financial planners joke that if you have enemies, give 'em a lottery ticket."[3]

AN INHERITANCE GAINED QUICKLY

I knew a woman and her new husband – I'll call them Betty and Henry – who, years ago, inherited around $250,000 from the death of Betty's mother. Betty had been a single mother, struggling to make ends meet. Henry was a self-employed handyman who could barely keep his business afloat. Both were kind, down-to-earth people.

The inheritance quickly changed everything.

As soon as Betty received her inheritance, Henry started spending the money to upgrade their lives. They bought new clothes, covered their fingers in expensive rings and their necks in precious metals, and bought new cars. They even upgraded their home – along with their mortgage.

They started walking with an air of sophistication, even snobbery; it didn't match who everyone knew them to be. Undoubtedly, they thought of themselves as different people. They developed an elitist mindset because they had now "arrived." *Where* they arrived, whatever that means, is up for debate.

Just like one third of the lottery winners, Betty and Henry eventually went bankrupt. They were worse off than they had ever been before. Plus, that season of delusion had alienated a lot of important people in their lives.

---

[3] Edelman, Rick (2016, Jan 15). *Why so many lottery winners go broke.* Retrieved from http://fortune.com/2016/01/15/powerball-lottery-winners/

We don't just do this with investments or lottery winnings. Plenty of people rationalize other financial decisions this way; for example, your career path.

After one of my full-day transformational leadership workshops in Atlanta, one of the participants stayed after to chat. That wasn't unusual, but what she *said* certainly was.

"Thank you for being with us today," said Mary. She looked as though she was still deep in thought. "The training was fabulous." I humbly received her compliments, but her next statement took me by surprise.

"Until now," she explained, "I didn't realize how greedy I have been. I was so focused on becoming an Internal Audit executive that it almost killed me."

"Seriously?" I asked, puzzled by her strong use of words. "What do you mean?"

"I finally achieved my career goal of becoming the VP of Internal Audit for this Fortune 500 company," she said with both a sense of pride and remorse. She was referring to the company that sponsored the event.

"Last year, I was forced to retire for health reasons," she went on. "My doctor said if I stayed in my position, it could eventually kill me. My husband pleaded with me to resign, so I did. I had just turned fifty." Mary looked down toward the floor, hesitant to meet my eyes.

Mary had contracted a rare condition called Sarcoidosis, an inflammatory disease that affects the internal organs. As she explained, "It basically eats away at my internal organs until they are destroyed."

No one knows how Sarcoidosis is contracted. But "stress can increase the misery caused by the disease."[4]

"The stress of my executive position was causing a lot of pain and was exacerbating my condition. I had no choice but to resign.

"But I realized today in your training that I placed so much of my identity in my career path that I've been feeling lost since I left. I put money and status above everything else in my life. It drove me to rise to the top. It almost drove me to my death. I was being greedy." She felt a clear sense of relief at this discovery.

Mary's blind spot almost killed her. Until you are able to handle the pain of facing *every* deception about yourself, you will never reach your fullest potential. You will never achieve the truest happiness you seek.

Mary found solace that day in knowing she no longer needed a title or large salary to feel important. She's now looking for other work that fulfills her without the high stress.

Workaholism is a cover up for a number of blind spots, not just materialism. When you heavily base your career trajectories on how much you will earn and how much prestige you will have, you open yourself up to these deceptions, these many blind spots that impact your behaviors and decision-making. It becomes all too easy to cross ethical boundaries.

You justify workaholism with excuses like, "I'm just working hard to provide a better lifestyle for my family; I want my kids to have a better life than I had growing up!" Or "I want to provide for my kids' college education." There are plenty of

---

[4] *Questions and Answers – The Disease.* Retrieved from http://sarcoid-network.org/FAQ/faq-disease.php

good reasons, but if they're hiding a blind spot then you get out of balance. You put yourself in a state of dissonance, and then rationalize to mitigate that dissonance.

The irony? Most of us think *we* will be less affected by money than the average person. We think that everyone *else* has the problem, but never us, right?

> *Blind Spot Challenge: Are you rationalizing your pursuit of wealth or career climb in order to reduce dissonance?*

COLLEGE CAREER

After graduating from high school, I enrolled in college with a pre-law emphasis. This wasn't because I fancied having "Esquire" after my name; it was because in my mind, attorneys earned a fortune. I wanted the money. The choice, therefore, was to either become a lawyer or a doctor. Those are the money-makers, right? And since I didn't have the stomach for dissecting frogs, the choice was easy.

College life was amazing! I made a ton of new friends, and we had loads of fun together. But, unfortunately, on my first day of classes, my counselor inadvertently placed me into a junior level law class. I was a freshman. What a disaster!

The first class lasted about 15 minutes. The professor assigned each of us roles in a mock trial., I would be the Assistant Prosecutor. Visions of Perry Mason danced through my head, until I realized how much work was involved. The glamour of courtroom dramas portrayed by Hollywood failed to show the countless hours of tedious, monotonous, hard work. Hopes shattered, I immediately dropped out of pre-law. To this day, I have a *lot* of respect for good attorneys and all they go through!

With all my other classes, studying always came at an inopportune time (doesn't it always?). It conflicted with my social life. So, after the first semester, I dropped out of college. I just don't think I was ready.

Not knowing what else to do, and craving a sense of purpose, I joined the United States Air National Guard. After basic and technical training, I returned home to my unit in Phoenix. There, I reported in on the weekends, but I needed a career for the in between. So, at my mother's encouragement, I enrolled in real estate school, and became a proud real estate sales professional.

REAL ESTATE AGENT

Within the first thirty days, I was fortunate to become an award-winning top producer, with a little help from my mother's guidance and generosity. I worked with her at Century 21[5]. The money was unbelievable. Life was amazing!

At nineteen, I purchased an almost-new four-door sedan with all the bells and whistles. I also bought a brand new, two-bedroom luxury condominium, complete with an expensive hi-definition stereo system and monster speakers. I'm sure my neighbors were thrilled! In the midst of all this, I met and started dating a young woman in modeling school. I was living the American Dream.

Well, at least I had the *appearance* of success; I was even on my way to becoming nationally recognized for it. But, despite the material gain, something felt wrong. I couldn't explain it; no matter how much "stuff" I acquired, or how successful I became, it felt something was still missing.

---

[5] Century 21, Realtor, Realtor.com and MLS are registered trademarks of their respective owners.

"Ah, maybe I just needed more adventure," I thought. "I'll never get it living so close to home. The Air National Guard was not the answer. Maybe I should call my recruiter and transfer to the full-time Air Force? Certainly, that will be an adventure. I could travel the world. Yes. That's what I'll do. First thing Monday."

And I did.

I suppose I could have just planned exotic vacations. Honestly, though, I needed structure as much as adventure. Switching to full-time active duty provided that, and came with a sense of community. It made sense at the time, and I'm still glad to be able to serve my country – if only for a season.

> *Blind Spot Challenge: What does true success look like to you and do your actions align with this belief?*

UNITED STATES AIR FORCE

The recruiter was thrilled to put in my request for active duty. When he asked where in the world I'd like to be stationed, he warned that the first assignment would likely be in the US, and that I'd better pick at least one or two locations here where I'd be satisfied living. I chose Germany, California and Colorado.

I figured if I couldn't find adventure in Europe, I would certainly find it on the beaches of California or the ski slopes in Colorado.

He explained it could take six months for an assignment to come through. We were both surprised when the orders arrived almost immediately. Two weeks later I packed my bags and headed off to McClellan Air Force Base in Sacramento, thrilled at the thought of the new experiences.

The first month on base was quite the adventure. I met more friends, started seeing someone, settled in to my new job assignment as an electronics radio repair technician, and was having the time of my life. It was like that first day of college, only better!

There was only one problem. That sense of emptiness deep in my soul kept cropping up. I thought the new adventure would fill the void, but it didn't. So, I did what I always did to quench the feelings that seemed like loneliness: I pulled out my trumpet.

I started playing trumpet in third grade. Whenever I felt that restlessness or emptiness in my soul, I could satisfy it, at least temporarily, by playing some good jazz or blues.

Since I lived in the dorms on base, I needed a safe and polite place to play. I found it a couple buildings down at the base post office, where the steps and portico leading in to the mailboxes provided a small shelter. Sometimes, late at night, I'd head over there to play without bothering anyone.

One evening while playing on those steps, I met Sargent Donna Martinez, a new friend who would prove to be another significant influence on my worldview.

THE INTUITION BLIND SPOT

She came walking up the steps and sat down.

"Hmm," I thought, "I never thought playing trumpet would be a chic-magnet." I shared with Donna why I was playing my trumpet; how it soothed the loneliness in my soul.

She wasn't buying it.

"Do you know the song *Amazing Grace*?" she asked.

"Of course," I said, with a sense of pride. "We played it in Jazz Band every once in a while."

I proceeded to dazzle her (or so I thought) with my talents.

After I finished the song, Donna didn't miss a beat: she looked me right in the eyes and said, as serious as a doctor giving a prognosis, "Kevin, God sent me over here to tell you about Jesus."

Her words sent a chill down my spine. For a moment, I felt like she was looking deep into my soul – but then, I wasn't convinced. *You mean the lunatic who talked to God and carried out his wishes?* I wondered.

On the other hand, I loved to philosophize about the meaning of life. So, I shrugged, *why not?*

"Let's have a discussion," I said with a smile.

Now, before I continue, let me assure my readers that this is not a religious or spiritual book. Rather, this moment is a critical part of the story that will help you understand my worldview during my crime, along with some blind spots we've yet to discuss.

I asked Donna all the questions I could think to ask. I thought I was throwing her curve balls by talking about aliens and UFO's, but she wasn't daunted in the slightest.

My family wasn't religious or spiritual. I didn't grow up in church. I only remember trying church once or twice as a kid, at Christmas or Easter. So, when Donna tried to use the Bible to explain my quest for truth – a quest I was not consciously aware I was even on – I didn't really give her much credence. On the other hand, I was amused and intrigued by the dialogue. Plus, the female company, of course, was part of a whole different quest.

As it turned out, Donna seemed to have all the answers to my questions; everything she said explained the void I was feeling in my soul. I was overwhelmed with satisfaction.

After two long discussions (or rather debates) over the course of two separate nights, with her ability to answer even my toughest questions, I bowed my head and made a spiritual decision that altered the course of my thinking. There was a strange peace that permeated every fiber of my being. I quickly became heavily involved and committed to her Christian church.

The spiritual decision I made is an Intuitive Blind Spot. I placed my trust for my eternity in Jesus Christ, and decided to live the rest of my life in the Christian faith – based on just a couple of conversations with one person! She was not a professed authority of ancient manuscripts; nor did she offer any empirical evidence of God's existence (a debate we won't discuss here). I did not do any research, or try and get other opinions. I simply made a decision based on my gut. It was an intuitive decision. It felt right at the time, and made sense in the context of what I felt I was missing. It was a decision I later questioned and rationally reevaluated, from inside a Federal prison.

Blind Spot Challenge: What beliefs do you hold or what decisions have you made strictly using intuition? Will they withstand being rationally challenged?

INTUITION

Intuition is important. In certain circumstances, quick intuitive decisions can save your life, like when you instinctively turn and walk the other way when an unsavory character walking towards you just doesn't seem quite right. But making intuition-based decisions can also lead you astray if you aren't careful.

In his book *Blink,* Malcolm Gladwell postulates that your *best* decisions are made intuitively, in an instant. He bases this theory, in part, on relatively new research called thin-slicing.

"*Thin-slicing* refers to the ability of our unconscious to find patterns in situations and behavior based on very narrow slices of experience.[6]"

In essence, thin-slicing is the unconscious process of perceiving events and stimuli through the framework of your worldview, then creating intuitive impressions, thoughts and feelings.

"Part of what it means to take thin-slicing and first impressions seriously is accepting the fact that sometimes you can know more about someone or something in the blink of an eye than you can after months of study. But you also have to acknowledge and understand those circumstances when rapid cognition leads you astray.[7]"

---

[6] Gladwell, Malcolm, *Blink*, Little, Brown and Company, 2005. Page 23, emphasis added.
[7] ibid, page 76

Though your "gut instinct" can at times be correct based on thin-slicing, it can also be just as incorrect. This is why you must evaluate your first impressions, intuitions and instincts rationally to determine if what you first determined is actually true. More on how you employ your rational thinking later, when we discuss Daniel Kahneman's System 1 and System 2.

EXPERT FALLACY

Thin-slicing can contribute to the Expert Fallacy. Since thin-slicing relies on drawing from your experience in an instant, the more experienced you are, or the more of an expert you are, the more you tend to rely on thin-slicing when called upon to assess a situation within your expertise.

The expert bias can cause good people to make bad choices when you shun, or completely miss, certain perspectives. You might *feel* like you know the solution, when in fact you have not looked at enough different perspectives to even challenge your own presuppositions.

The expert fallacy can cause companies to continue with a culture of business as usual. After all, the experts who started and lead the company should certainly know what's best, right? Maybe. But not if they are unaware of their blind spots.

Experts have the toughest time dealing with pride and arrogance. If they remain humble and aware, they can continue to be adaptable, look for new perspectives, and lead their companies to new heights as times change.

Entire industries can be affected by the expert fallacy. The Taxi industry never predicted the impact of Uber or Lyft, the hospitality industry was totally blindsided by AirBnB?

It's no longer business as usual.

Blind Spot Challenge: When is the last time you tested your expert assumptions with new perspectives and up-dated research?

SERIAL ENTREPRENEUR

There were several reasons I left the Air Force, but the number one reason was money. When I was trying to decide whether to remain in the military or move on to the private sector, I followed the advice of Rusty Johnson, a man who (at the time) was an important spiritual role model for me.

Rusty's comment pushed me over the fence: "Kevin, I see you as a guy who will generate much money through the work of your hands. I don't see that as possible if you remain in the military."

I didn't know it at the time, but he played a significant role in strengthening my worldview and the pursuit of wealth. Ironically, I don't think he realized how much influence he would have on my "love of money."

So, without any further thought or counsel, again based almost entirely on an encouraging comment from someone I esteemed, I left the military to pursue the American Dream.

There were two blind spots at play here. One was the Celebrity Blind Spot; the other was Confirmation Bias.

CELEBRITY BLIND SPOT

Rusty was a celebrity to me. He was an international speaker in the church world, and was a guest speaker for our local church the weekend we met. He certainly seemed like someone to be admired, especially considering how young and impressionable I was.

So, when he made that comment, I was easily convinced his advice was sound.

Good people make bad choices when you are more easily influenced by people you put on pedestals. You unconsciously allow them to have significantly more influence than is logically warranted. This is why Hollywood celebrities are sought after to endorse products or services. The celebrity might have zero expertise as a financial planner, but when he's seen endorsing a financial planning brand on television, people are persuaded.

When I was twenty-four, I signed up to be an independent distributor for a nutritional product company. How did I make that decision? Well, this company contracted William Shatner, who played Captain James T. Kirk of the U.S.S. Enterprise in the *Star Trek* series, as their spokesperson. All I needed was good ol' Captain Kirk's endorsement; since he was my childhood hero and could do no wrong, the company must be solid, right?

Definitely *not!*

| *Blind Spot Challenge: Who are you allowing to influence your life and decisions?*

Placing people on a pedestal, esteeming them, and allowing them to influence you is not always a bad thing. If the person has earned the right to influence you, by all means they should be able to. After all, we can all learn valuable lessons about service from someone like Mother Theresa. But allowing Captain Kirk to influence your decision to do business with a nutritional company? Not so much.

CONFIRMATION BIAS

Confirmation Bias plays a significant role in good people making bad choices. It certainly played a role in my decision to follow Rusty's advice. I already wanted to separate from the Air Force, so when he *confirmed* what I was thinking, it was easy to act on his advice.

"Confirmation bias refers to a type of selective thinking whereby one tends to notice and look for information that confirms one's current beliefs; they may also ignore, not look for, or undervalue the relevance of information that contradicts one's beliefs."[8]

When it comes to making decisions, *ScienceDaily* describes confirmation bias as "a phenomenon wherein decision makers have been shown to actively seek out and assign more weight to evidence that confirms their hypothesis, and ignore or under weigh evidence that could disconfirm their hypothesis."[9]

In its simplest form, this is like, If Mom says 'no', ask Dad. You're probably going to ask the parent you know will say yes.

Sir Francis Bacon described it this way: "The human understanding, when it has once adopted an opinion (either as being the received opinion or as being agreeable to itself) draws all things else to support and agree with it."[10]

We see this operating in our religious beliefs. Often, when you adhere to a specific religious group, you look for evidence that supports what you already believe. You tend to ignore evi-

---

[8] Retrieved from http://skepdic.com/confirmbias.html
[9] Retrieved from
https://www.sciencedaily.com/terms/confirmation_bias.htm
[10] Bacon, F. (1939). Novum organum. In Burtt, E. A. (Ed.), The English philosophers from Bacon to Mill (p. 36). New York: Random House. (Original work published in 1620)

dence that might be contrary to your belief, even if the opposing evidence outweighs the supporting evidence.

Take global warming as an example. There are extreme views from scientists on both sides of the argument.[11] According to Matt Ridley, who ran a three-column *Wall Street Journal* series on the topic of scientific confirmation bias, culminating with an article titled: "How Bias Heats Up the [Global] Warming Debate," apparently, "Scientists are just as prone to confirmation bias as everybody else...a tendency to look for evidence to support rather than test your own ideas."[12]

Confirmation bias can be helpful to create healthy debates and cause others to challenge your beliefs. You just need to make sure you're not shutting out those who oppose your beliefs. You need to look for feedback or data in areas that might not necessarily support your beliefs or desires.

If you want to remain as neutral as possible while you gather data and make decisions, you need to remain aware of your own confirmation bias to reduce its effects.

> *Blind Spot Challenge: What beliefs or desires are you holding so tightly that you might become a victim of confirmation bias?*

---

[11] Something to consider: While there are extreme POLITICAL views on both sides of the Climate Change debate, the scientific community is in strong consensus, more than 95%, that the earth is warming, and that it is anthropogenic; the same level of confidence with which we say "Smoking causes cancer." (I have no opinion in this matter since I have not invested nor desire to invest the time to research both sides of the argument.)

[12] Bell, Larry (2012, Aug 14). *Confirmation bias: Why both sides of the global warming debate are nearly always right.* Retrieved from
http://www.forbes.com/sites/larrybell/2012/08/14/confirmation-bias-why-both-sides-of-the-global-warming-debate-are-nearly-always-right/#701a444a4b1d

THE GRASS IS GREENER SYNDROME

After leaving the Air Force, I was hired as a salesman at Valley Ford, a local Ford dealership. After training, I quickly became an award-winning top producer for the company, back to enjoying an upper-middle-class lifestyle.

However, after about one year at Valley Ford, I felt I was peaking out financially.

"Selling imports is where all the money is, Kev!" a fellow sales professional chided.

"Yeah, that's what I hear," I said, but asked him curiously: "It's tough getting into those dealerships, isn't it?"

"Well, if you can keep a secret, I'm leaving here next week to work for Harrison Toyota," he said. "I'll put in a good word for you."

To my surprise, he actually did. I didn't think much about it at the time, but the following Friday afternoon I received a call at work from the sales manager at Toyota.

"Hi, Kevin," a voice on the other line began in a hurry. "This is Mark from Harrison Toyota. I was told that you are a top producer looking to step up your game. I have one opening on my crew. Interested?"

"Absolutely!" I said, trying to restrain my enthusiasm. "I would love to be on your crew. When do I start?"

"Immediately," he quipped. "How fast can you be here? You start now. It's Friday night and my shift has already begun. We close tonight."

"Oh, uh, that's a bit too soon," I said nervously. "I'm on

duty here at Ford the rest of the evening. I'd also like to give at least a week's notice," I added. "Would that work?"

"Nope!" Mark said without skipping a beat. "This is a one-time offer. Take it or leave it. Be here in thirty minutes or I'll find someone else."

Talk about rushed! I didn't want to lose the opportunity for advancement, but I didn't want to just walk out on my current boss. What could I do?

"Okay, Mark," I said, making a sudden decision. "I'll be right over. Thanks!"

I told my current boss I wasn't feeling well and had to leave. I felt terrible about lying to him, but I didn't have the heart to just quit and tell him I was going to work for his competitor.

I started working for Harrison Toyota that night. At first, I was elated. I felt like I'd moved up to the big boys' game in car sales, and unfortunately, I really had. It was a brutal experience at which I failed miserably.

Working for a family-owned Ford dealership with a great reputation for honesty and customer service had sheltered me from the "real world" of car sales. Customers at Valley Ford were treated with integrity. I felt good about myself in every transaction.

In contrast, I spent six weeks at Harrison Toyota. They sold the most in-demand products on the market, and they sold a lot of them. The problem was, the managers and crew at this particular dealership had no scruples. The attitude was, "Roll the car no matter what." Salespeople would say whatever it took to get the paperwork signed – once the car left the lot, it wasn't the dealership's problem. I simply couldn't handle the pressure or the ethics.

I refused to play the game. As a result, I earned a total of three hundred dollars during those six weeks, which didn't compare with the $900-1,000 plus per week I earned as a top producer at Ford.

Unfortunately, there was no returning to the Ford dealership. On my first night at the Toyota dealership I met a potential customer and showed them around the lot. They didn't find a car they liked and said they were going to check out Valley Ford. So, trying to help them out, I referred them to one of the salespeople there who I knew would treat them fairly. I never saw the next conversation coming!

About an hour after referring the customer, I heard my name over the loud speaker at Toyota.

"Kevin McCarthy, customer call on line 2."

Excited that I was already receiving inquiries, I rushed back into the showroom and grabbed the first phone I could find.

"Hi, this is Kevin," I said with eager anticipation.

"Kevin, this is Sebastian. What the hell are you doing at Toyota? I thought you were sick!" It was the sales manager at Valley Ford, and he was angry.

I explained about the sudden job offer, and apologized for lying. I felt horrible. Sebastian had been good to me -- he deserved a better exit. He made it clear that I was not welcome back.

I experienced the Pressure Blind spot, and paid the price.

THE PRESSURE BLIND SPOT

When making decisions, you need to be keenly aware of any pressures. Mark was a master sales closer. He knew how much I wanted to make the move, so he went for the take-it-or-leave-it close. That is, he applied an incredible amount of pressure on me to make an immediate decision. I succumbed to the deception that I didn't have time to think about it and seek counsel from others, or do the right thing. I wanted the advancement opportunity, and Mark knew it, so, he exploited it.

I don't blame Mark for my demise in car sales. I was greedy, and I believed the rumors about imports. I made poor decisions in the way I handled the transition from one dealership to the other. What's more, I *knew* I was making some poor choices, but made them anyway.

Some car salespeople are trained to exert extreme pressure on potential customers. They know that poor decisions can be influenced under pressure. Always avoid salespeople who apply pressure to your decision. Take your time. Don't feel rushed. A well-trained, professional salesperson will masterfully persuade without resorting to pressure tactics. An ethical sales professional will only persuade buyers if the purchase will be good for the *buyer*, not just the salesperson's paycheck.

Action Tip: Resist major purchases when you sense the pressure to buy now.

External pressures are often easier to identify than internal pressures. It might sound easier to recognize a high-pressure sales tactic and push back, but when the external pressure triggers an unconscious internal pressure…well, as they say, *Caveat Emptor* – Buyer Beware.

"For instance, it's been recognized for several decades that people are more sensitive to losses than to gains, a phenomenon known as *loss aversion*. This doesn't fit with economic theory[13], but it appears to be hard-wired into the brain."[14]

In other words, the external pressure from the salesperson may trigger an internal pressure of *not wanting someone else to buy this car* since you like it so much. Your emotions about the car guide your decision to succumb to the pressure.

When salespeople feel intense pressure from their managers, spoken or unspoken, to meet quotas or potentially lose their jobs, they tend to make poor decisions, even when those decisions would appear, at least in hindsight, to be completely unethical. Consider the Wells Fargo fiasco in 2016: 5,300 people were fired for creating more than 2 million phony accounts.[15]

Internal auditors, according to the Association of Certified Fraud Examiners, are supposed to "provide an independent and objective assessment of the effectiveness and efficiency of a company's operations, specifically its internal control structure.[16]"

However, occasionally internal auditors feel pressure from management, executives, and general counsel. According to the *Wall Street Journal*, "Nearly one in four internal auditors

---

[13] Economic theory is a broad concept for the explanation and understanding of the movement of goods in a market. http://www.wisegeek.com/what-is-economic-theory.htm

[14] Sanfey, Alan G. & Chang, Luke J. (2008, Jun 3). *Of two minds when making a decision*. Retrieved from https://www.scientificamerican.com/article/of-two-minds-when-making/

[15] Egan, Matt (2016, Sep 9). *5,300 Wells Fargo employees fired over 2 million phony accounts*. Retrieved from http://money.cnn.com/2016/09/08/investing/wells-fargo-created-phony-accounts-bank-fees/

[16] Retrieved from http://www.acfe.com/career-path-internal-auditor.aspx

surveyed globally by The Internal Audit Foundation said they've been pressured to suppress or change their findings."[17]

It's important for auditors to understand that even though the company might employ them, they must act independently and objectively, regardless of the potential outcome.

Even if an auditor is not directly asked to leave out key information, internal auditors can feel the pressure to complete a certain number of audits in an unreasonable amount of time, and rush the process. Or, they might spend too much time on lower priority controls and suffer undue pressure to complete the more important ones.

THE FRAUD TRIANGLE

Pressure is one of the three components that make up what fraud examiners refer to as the Fraud Triangle[18].

The Fraud triangle is a framework designed to explain the reasoning behind a worker's decision to commit fraud and embezzlement. The three stages, categorized by the effect on the individual, can be summarized as pressure, opportunity and rationalization.[19]

In other words, when good people feel intense financial pressures and recognize an opportunity, they might find themselves rationalizing what would normally be recognized as a terrible decision.

---

[17] Shumsky, Tatyana (2016, Nov 1). *Nearly a quarter of internal auditors report pressure to suppress their findings.* Retrieved from
http://blogs.wsj.com/cfo/2016/11/01/nearly-a-quarter-of-internal-auditors-report-pressure-to-suppress-their-findings/

[18] Cressey, Donald R., *Other People's Money*, Montclair: Patterson Smith, 1973, pg 30.

[19] *What is the fraud triangle?* Retrieved from http://www.hrzone.com/hr-glossary/what-is-the-fraud-triangle

I met a man in prison who told me he was a former Bank of America branch manager. Mark had a beautiful wife and two young, athletic children. He coached his son's soccer league, lived in a middle-class neighborhood and owned a couple of affordable, fairly new, vehicles. He was esteemed in his community, living the American Dream. You would never know by looking at him that Mark embezzled more than $300,000 from his bank branch.

Mark felt extreme internal pressure to keep up the façade of success. Meanwhile, he was drowning in debt and living way beyond his means. He knew something had to happen, or the lifestyle he created would completely fall apart. He feared the ridicule and shame of being seen as a failure if he couldn't keep up the pace.

Then one day, as Mark was reviewing client accounts, he noticed one corporate account, with a substantial balance, that appeared to be dormant. A larger conglomerate had recently purchased the company.

He described what happened.

"Well Kev, I was just really stupid," he said with a tremendous look of guilt and shame.

"There I was, sitting at my desk. I felt like I was going to have a nervous breakdown from all the financial pressures I'd created.

"I was reviewing client accounts that morning when I noticed this dormant account – with over one million dollars, just sitting there! The new company had missed it during the acquisition. That realization triggered a chain reaction I'll always regret.

"I thought to myself, 'nobody knows this money is sitting

here. So, no one will notice if it goes missing.' That's all it took. and I figured out how to slowly siphon off the money."

"Mark –" I had to interject at this point – "didn't you realize you were committing a serious crime, and could go to jail?"

"The thought crossed my mind for a second," he admitted. "But I was able to convince myself that the company would never miss the money...and that I was clever enough to help myself to it without being noticed. Boy, was I wrong!"

Mark took the money incrementally over fifteen months, and mostly used it to maintain his lifestyle. He was caught on his last attempt, during which he was helping himself to another $40,000.

Mark received a 29-month sentence and five years of supervised release. Several weeks after he arrived at the prison, his wife and children came to visit. She told him it would be her last. She filed for divorce.

Mark was a good man who made a bad choice. He paid a high price.

The pressures that affect your decisions can be external or internal, and sometimes you get both. When these pressures exist and go unrecognized, your decisions are impacted.

Even when you *think* you are aware of the pressures, you don't necessarily recognize how intensely pressure affects your decisions.

> *Action Tip: When making important decisions, stop long enough to evaluate any external or internal pressures. Then factor them into the decision.*

Beware of the Pressure Blind Spot!

IN PURSUIT OF WEALTH

As I was leaving the Air Force, I met Rachel, the love of my life. I asked her to marry me on our very first date, and she said "yes." It was divine intervention! I can't think of a better way to explain it.

It was August 1985. I was single and living in the Sacramento area. I was attending a small home group study with our church when our pastor, Garry, made the announcement:

"Hey everyone, Jody [his wife] and I are excited to tell you that we have hired someone to help us part time in the ministry. Her name is Rachel. She just graduated college and is moving here from Oregon."

Garry went on to provide more details of what her role would be and how she would obtain a second part time job since the church couldn't afford her full time. While he was talking, I had this crazy thought run through my head.

"This woman is going to be your wife."

I immediately discounted the thought as a crazy fantasy. I had never heard of Rachel before the announcement, let alone met her. How could I possibly assume I would marry her?

Rachel arrived two weeks later and attended her first church service. She was – and still is – a beautiful blonde with a kind face and radiant smile that lights up any room she enters. Many of us took a moment to welcome her, and as soon as I shook her hand that same thought popped into my head again:

"This woman is going to be your wife."

"This is crazy!" I thought, and shrugged it off once more.

Over the next few months, Rachel and I started to become friends. As it turns out, we had a number of things in common; we both played brass instruments in high school bands and were both guitar players and singers.

Around mid-November 1985, that thought kept coming back. I really felt like it might be God speaking to me directly. I could not resist any longer – I needed to say something. Then again, I was terrified to mention it to Rachel for fear of ruining a friendship. So instead, I visited Garry and told him what I was thinking.

"Kevin," he said in a fatherly, loving-but-stern voice. "Don't you dare tell Rachel. That would be manipulative to tell her that God wants her to marry you. Just let this go and trust God. If he is prompting you, I'm sure he can work it out with Rachel. Can you do that?"

"Sure, Garry. I actually made a deal with God." I felt silly even saying it, but I continued, "I told God that if he wanted me to marry Rachel, three things would have to happen. First, he would have to put a love in my heart for her since I don't love her that way. Second, he would have to build our friendship because I am going to withdraw from it as much as possible. And, finally, he would have to tell Rachel, because I am never going to do that!"

Garry laughed. "Perfect! Jody and I will be praying for you and this situation. Just keep this to yourself."

Over the next couple of months, as much as I tried to withdraw, circumstances kept bringing Rachel and me together. For example, the church members were planning a Christmas party, so, at an earlier gathering, Garry passed a hat around for us to draw names for a gift exchange. He walked to each person and held his baseball hat above our heads. We reached in and grabbed a piece of paper. When it was my turn, I reached in and...

"Oh, my goodness! This is unbelievable!" I thought to myself. I picked "Rachel." I could hardly contain myself with the irony. These types of crazy things kept happening to us over the next few months.

Several of us went to a concert, and after it was over Rachel discovered she had locked her keys in her car. It just so happened that I was the only person left to help her unlock the door with a coat hanger. Then, on another occasion, about twelve friends gathered at a theater to watch a movie. Since I love the end seat, I stood by the row ushering people into the row. Rachel happened to be the last person to sit down – right next to me. It was awkward!

Finally, on February 5, 1986 at a small church gathering in Garry and Jody's home, Garry asked to talk with me.

We walked out onto his backyard patio. "How are you feeling about this thing with Rachel?" he asked, clearly curious.

My answer spoke of a conviction that had been growing. "Garry, this may sound crazy, but I have such a love in my heart for her that even if it takes ten years for her to hear the same thing I heard, I will wait."

No matter how I tried to pull away from the friendship, love was welling up in my heart. I quit fighting it. But, I had honored Garry's advice and committed to not telling Rachel – at least not prematurely.

Garry started laughing. "Well brother, you just need to do what you need to do now! About two weeks ago, Jodi and Rachel were talking, and Rachel said that when she was praying, she felt like the Lord spoke to her that she was going to marry you! I think now, it's all up to you."

I couldn't believe my ears. I was so excited. I could hardly wait to say something to Rachel. I quickly walked back in the house and approached her.

"Hey, I just heard from Garry about your conversation with Jody. Would you like to go out to dinner with me tomorrow night?"

Without hesitation, she accepted.

The next evening, I picked her up and we drove to an Italian restaurant in Sacramento. Once we were seated and placed our orders, I got up from my seat, kneeled on the floor in front of the table, and sang Rachel a marriage proposal I had written. Listen, if this was really divine, why should I waste time, right?

With tears in her eyes, she said "Yes!"

We were married six months later in August 1986, and have lived happily ever after! Well, okay... that's a *slight* exaggeration. We've had plenty of rough patches and continue to work through our own blind spots. But I'm happy to report that we celebrated our 30th anniversary in 2016, and look forward to many more.

Over the next several years I worked at a Savings and Loan, started a cellular retail store, purchased and later sold a hair salon, and started a Century 21 real estate franchise. I was the consummate entrepreneur in search of financial independence, still completely unaware of my Materialism and Generosity Blind Spots.

CENTURY 21 SUCCESS!

In 1988, together with my mother, Judi, and a good friend, John, we opened a Century 21 real estate franchise in Mesa, Arizona, just before the real estate market rebounded. With only three of us to occupy it, we rented and improved a 7,300-square-foot retail space on the busiest intersection in the city.

With our business plan and a little dumb luck, in just under two years we became the number one Century 21 franchise in Arizona. Within five years, we were ranked 13th largest in the country, out of more than 6,000 franchises.

This notoriety led to an invitation to serve on the Board of Directors for the Maricopa County Brokers Council, a group comprised at the time of thirty-one independent Century 21 franchisees.

At thirty-one years old, I was the youngest Board member and quite possibly the youngest franchisee in the area.

WHAT IS THIS INTERNET THING?

In 1994, at one of our Council meetings, we were all discussing the Internet. That's when I asked a question that changed the course of my career.

"So, what do you think this Internet *thing* will do to our real estate businesses?" I asked candidly.

They all stared blankly until one of the members spoke up.

"I have no idea," he said jokingly. "Why don't you figure it out and let us all know?"

I took on the challenge.

Over the next couple of months, I spent more than 100 hours researching the Internet and its potential impact on the real estate industry. My research led me to believe that creating a website to showcase all of our Century 21 offices and agents would be smart marketing. It also seemed that as consumers caught on, they would want to search for available homes right from their screen. We needed to figure out how to keep a fresh inventory of homes on our site for the hundreds of agents who worked for the 31 franchisees. I had to figure out a way to bridge the gap between building the website, ongoing maintenance, and the Multiple Listing Service (MLS) that maintained a real-time database of all the homes for sale in the market area. It was a daunting task, but I cracked the code.

Knowing that at the next meeting I would need to present a solid plan and budget to the Council, I secured three bids from different web hosting companies in the area. I then presented my exciting discovery to the members for a vote. It was unanimous: the council decided to spend almost all of the money in our reserves to be first to market with this revolutionary idea.

After the meeting, Dale Dalmer, the Regional Vice President for the Southwest division of Century 21, approached me.

"Kevin, I don't know what magic you had in your presentation," he said with amazement, "but no one in the history of this council has ever received a unanimous vote to spend such a sizeable amount of money, let alone most of the cash on hand."

He then said, "Would you consider being my keynote speaker for five of our upcoming sales rallies throughout the Southwest region? I'll pay you five hundred dollars per event, plus your travel costs."

I was dumbfounded. I couldn't even believe people got

paid to speak, especially amateurs like me. So, of course I agreed. "Yes!" I said. "I'd love to do that."

A NEW SPEAKING CAREER

A couple months later, I shared my thoughts at these sales rallies on how the World Wide Web would impact the real estate industry. It was exhilarating! The tour led to a 14-state speaking arrangement with the Century 21 Western Division, and eventually I went national. I traveled to every state on multiple occasions, teaching real estate audiences how to brand and market themselves on the web. I was having so much fun helping people grow their businesses that I sold my own real estate company.

Meanwhile, the Broker's Council had the website developed per the plan. It was the first site of its kind, listing all of the homes for sale in real-time, directly from the MLS.

Six months after we launched the site, the National Association of Realtors announced it had its own national branded website, Realtor.com. It *also* included all the home listings from the various MLS systems, so our local Broker's Council rightly voted to scrap our project and jump on the national platform.

While speaking to thousands of real estate professionals throughout North America, I kept hearing a common theme: though they liked what Realtor.com had to offer, they wanted to be able to differentiate and customize their own online profile.

A SMALL DOT COM COMPANY

Responding to this feedback, I modified the original website tech plan I'd presented to the Broker's Council. Now, it included semi-customization features for agents, and I offered these instant and semi-customizable websites for $49.95 per month, with a one-time $100 set up fee.

The demand was overwhelming. I had inadvertently created a new technology company as an adjunct to speaking and training. It was awesome! I called it the Real Estate Technology Institute – RETI[20] for short. We provided web solutions, speaking and training, and we grew rapidly both in customer base and staff.

In 1999, while attending the annual trade show for the National Association of Realtors, we were approached by Homeseekers.com. The principles wanted to fly me to California to discuss purchasing RETI.

Of course, I accepted. This is what I lived for: the opportunity to develop and sell a company. I was full to the brim with excitement as I prepared to take the trip.

A week later, I sat in the office of John Giamo, the President of Homeseekers.com, and Doug Swanson, the Vice-chairman of the Board. This was a publicly held company with stock trading on the NASDAQ. I felt like I was living a dream.

After a couple hours of getting to know each other, he and Doug made me an offer I couldn't refuse. It was a substantial sum of cash and stock combined, plus the opportunity to run a division within the company.

Even though I enjoyed building businesses, I was tired of always being undercapitalized and working long hours. So, what Doug said next, even more than the money, spoke volumes, and really sealed the deal.

---

[20] I am grateful for my RETI business partner, Eddie Morris who continues to remain a true friend.

"Kevin, we don't really care how many hundreds of clients you have. We are buying you. We believe you are the right guy to help us grow our business. You will have all the financial and human resources you need to run a successful division. How does that sound?"

I started crying.

In spite of the outward appearance of success, I was secretly craving a sabbatical – a six-month retreat away from the pace and pressures of business. I needed time away from people and technology to reset and refresh. I was experiencing burnout. Doug had no idea that his offer came at the perfect time. I might not be getting my six-month break, but the idea that I was no longer undercapitalized was exhilarating.

I accepted.

I felt like I had finally "arrived." As a small business entrepreneur, I was always trying to find the formula that would fulfill that childhood dream of "being rich."

The next nine months as the President of the broker division of Homeseekers.com felt like I was living on cloud nine. I grew the division to 54 people, made up mostly of sales professionals and managers who could handle various regions throughout the country.

We were on the verge of launching a new, national product line when the bad news arrived.

THE BELLAGIO PHONE CALL

I was hosting a management retreat in Las Vegas. These events were always fun; we got to sleep and eat at the Bellagio. As we

all walked to dinner, I received a phone call from Doug that put a dent in our mood.

"Kevin, whatever you do, do not sell your stock. It will hurt the company," he said with panic in his voice.

"Doug, what are you talking about?" I was completely perplexed by the call, and those intense opening comments.

We were in the middle of a planning session with visions of national sales dancing in our heads; we had no idea that the dot-com bubble had burst. Wall street was in a frenzy. So were Doug and the rest of the team.

"An investor, who promised us ten million dollars, just pulled out," Doug explained frantically. "Funding sources have dried up. No one is willing to commit the resources we need at the moment. I'm sure we'll make it through this blip. I just called to say hang on to your stocks. If the market sees our leadership selling off stock portfolios, we'll sink. Okay?"

"No problem, Doug. I trust your judgment." And I did. I really did.

So much so, in fact, that I relayed the message to my two good friends who also had significant shares in the Homeseekers.com. They followed my lead, and we all held on to our stock in solidarity.

What we didn't know was that Doug's best friend, also a significant shareholder, sold his entire portfolio immediately to amass a fortune in cash before the market finally crashed.

Homeseekers.com could not withstand the hit. It eventually went out of business, and we all lost our stock. The wealth I thought I had achieved was gone.

Why did I listen to Doug and not seek outside council?

Well, I was loyal and trusting. Only later would I discover that I had a severe Loyalty Blind Spot.

THE LOYALTY BLIND SPOT

Loyalty is a virtue. However, like any virtue, there are extremes on both sides. A deficiency of loyalty is unfaithfulness, but an excess of loyalty is fanaticism. I didn't know it at the time, but while I thought of myself as a loyal person, I was actually fanatical. I was loyal to a fault.

To truly be healthy, loyalty must be self-examined and balanced. You must reason through your various loyalties and decide to what degree you will maintain them. When you do not reason through the boundaries of your loyalties, you have a blind spot that can easily be exploited.

I never stopped to reason through my loyalties to Homeseekers.com. Frankly, it never crossed my mind, like it probably never crossed yours. When Doug said to not sell my stock so the company wouldn't be harmed, I blindly carried out his wishes as a loyal executive.

How loyal should you be? It depends on the time, place and person. You decide.

In this case, loyalty to the company should not have exceeded loyalty to my family. It can certainly be a fine line of reasoning, can't it? For instance, was loyalty to the company *serving* loyalty to my family? Maybe, but that still smacks of rationalization and workaholism. Even if I had been aware of the Loyalty Blind spot, I still might have rationalized my decision.

At the very least, I should have recognized the dilemma and had a conversation with Rachel about the decision. I owed her a higher degree of loyalty than I did to Doug or the company, that I didn't see in the moment.

Should you be loyal to your spouse? The obvious answer is yes, but to what degree? Ask your spouse if you should be loyal enough to never share your affections with anyone else and he or she will emphatically say, "YES!" But if your husband is physically assaulting you, should you still remain loyal? If he is placing your children in harm's way because of physical abuse, should you still remain loyal? Most people would say "no." Yet many women remain in this situation far too long.

Consider your different loyalties; reason through the degrees to which you should or should not remain loyal. Most importantly, do this *before* you find yourself forced to make a sudden decision. Knowing your loyalty boundaries will help you make strong decisions when the situation calls for it.

CHAPTER THREE:
WE'RE GOING TO BE RICH!

COFFEE WITH WES

My position with Homeseekers.com ended the summer of 2000, just months before the company went under. They were frantically closing divisions to save themselves – mine included. Thankfully, summer in Seattle is a great time to be unemployed. The weather is beautiful, and most of those famous coffee shops have plenty of outdoor seating.

That summer, I met weekly at one of these coffee shops with Wes, a buddy from church. He was a sharp-dressed, successful entrepreneur who always seemed to have a pulse on the marketplace.

I'll never forget the day I first heard about Lawrence and his company. The sun was shining, and Wes and I sat together at a black metal table under a green umbrella, which almost managed to keep the sun from blinding us. We were sipping on our whipped iced coffee when Wes brought up the million-dollar question.

"So, Kevin, what are you going to do now?"

"Well," I said thoughtfully, "I think I'm going to start another real estate company. I'm working on a game plan."

"Do you have the funds left from your Homeseekers.com stock to finance a startup?" he asked, clearly puzzled.

"Well, not really. We lost most of our portfolio. I do have enough to keep us afloat for about three months, but I'll need to find a backer."

THE OPPORTUNITY

"Well, listen," Wes continued, getting excited. "You know I'm invested in five different IPO's. One of them is getting ready to go public in just a few months. It's supposed to be a huge offering on Wall Street. The treasurer of the company, Conrad, is a good friend, so if you'd like, I can ask him if you can buy some stock in the company through the friends-and-family-round." Wes's expression was eager; he looked me squarely in the eyes, obviously wanting to help. I was touched.

"Wow, Wes! You would do that favor for me?" I asked. "Can you tell me more about the company?"

He grinned and went on: "The company is called Health Maintenance Centers, or HMC for short; Lawrence, the CEO, founded it six years ago. It's an integrated preventative health care company with revolutionary technology that helps doctors prescribe and electronically monitor exercise and nutritional programs. It's really amazing, actually. When they go public, the new, trendier name will be Znetix.

"Lawrence had so much interest in the company that he's getting ready to go nationwide, and offer shares on the stock market.

"They've been raising millions through a friends-and-family stock offering, but are now poised to open on the NASDAQ in just a few months.

"So, what does an investment look like for me?" My minor skepticism was quickly drowned out by his enthusiastic response.

"Let me check with the treasurer before I give you any more details," he said. "I don't want to speak out of school."

I agreed to patiently wait for the details, and did my best to not get too excited as we left the coffee shop.

The Investment

It didn't take long. Within an hour, Wes called.

"Kevin, dude, I'm so stoked for you," he exclaimed. "Conrad agreed to slip you in at the last minute to the friends-and-family round. They are finalizing everything for the public offering, so, he's doing me a huge favor getting you in."

"Wes, that's awesome! How much will this cost, and what type of return should I expect?" I was trying hard to restrain the full extent of my excitement. I did harbor a small amount of skepticism – it sounded a bit too good to be true. But Wes was a good friend; he was *very* convincing, and it seemed like a dream come true!

"Conrad said he can only authorize up to 10,000 shares of stock for you," Wes explained, "at $1.00 per share. The price is expected to open on Wall Street around $18 to $22 per share."

"What? My $10,000 investment could be worth as much as $220,000 in just a couple months?" I was beside myself, but I wanted to be smart about this. "Can I meet the treasurer before making a final decision?"

Conrad was a young man in his late twenties, who agreed to meet that very afternoon. Wes pointed to Conrad's Mercedes when we walked into his office. Impressive, right?

Well, so was Conrad himself. He was sharply dressed and sounded, by all accounts, brilliant. I asked every question I could think to ask about the company and the investment.

Conrad explained how Shaquille O'Neal, Kobe Bryant and

other major sports figures were involved in the company. The former head of the International Olympic Committee, Dr. Charles Dillman, would be the new CEO of the public company.

I have no way of knowing if Conrad was telling me the truth that day. Company reps used these names plenty of times to promote sales (see Celebrity Bias, above) and I had seen Shaq at a party once (we'll get to that soon). In any case, I was impressed, and since Rachel had left all the stock investments up to me, I immediately wrote a check for $10,000. I was completely thrilled that the windfall from this public offering would fund my new real estate company, and knew I'd soon be back on my game.

CHOICE-SUPPORTIVE BLIND SPOT

Now that I had invested, I needed to convince myself that what I'd just done was a good thing. This is called the Choice-Supportive Blind Spot. It's a cognitive bias where you retroactively attribute as many positive attributes as possible to a decision you've already made. This helps reduce what is commonly known as Buyer's Remorse: that uncomfortable feeling you get after making a major purchase. People often experience this when buying automobiles. Once you leave the dealership and the reality of how much money you've spent sinks in, you might have a tendency to question whether your decision was wise. Of course, you don't *want* to feel like you've made a bad decision, so you justify it using the Choice-Supportive Blind Spot. You focus on every positive attribute and ignore any possible negative attributes of that decision.

Now that I was the owner of 10,000 shares in a company I knew *very* little about, I needed to justify my decision.

I spent the next few months researching anything and everything I could find about the company. It was not difficult.

The company had huge billboards inside Safeco Field, where the Seattle Mariners play. There were articles and press releases in the newspaper, all about this company and its purchasing of other companies.

There was a lot of chatter about the company on Internet bulletin boards like RagingBull.com. Most of the people posting comments were shareholders, and most of the comments were enthusiastic.

Sure, there were a few negative comments from investors who had been around for a few years. They seemed disillusioned that the pending IPO was taking so long to get to market, but I chalked that up to impatient investors blowing off steam. No big deal, right? The majority of posts were positive!

The more I researched, the more excited I got about the investment. The Choice-Supportive Blind Spot worked perfectly to put my mind at ease!

> *Blind Spot Challenge: Before you make a major decision, ask yourself what other research you need to do. Alas, after you make the decision, you will still be inclined to justify it with the Choice-Supportive Blind Spot.*

In September 2000, about three months after I made the investment, I received an excited call from Wes.

"Hey Kev, gotta minute?" he asked. He sounded like he couldn't wait to share some news.

"Sure, Wes. What's up?"

"Dude, Conrad mentioned your business development

background to Lawrence, and now Lawrence wants to speak with *you* about a consulting project! Can I give him your number?" Wes could hardly contain himself.

"Seriously, Wes? That's amazing! Well, I mean, I'm pretty busy with these real estate company plans. But, sure, have him give me a call."

I was acting coy. The truth is, I was over the moon that the CEO of this soon-to-be-multi-billion-dollar company wanted to chat with *me* about a project!

THE CALL FROM THE CEO

Later that afternoon, I was on my way home after running a few errands. My cell phone rang – it was Lawrence!

"Hi, this is Kevin," I said, trying to be as calm as possible.

"Kevin, this is Lawrence, the CEO of Health Maintenance Centers. Wes gave me your number. I need your help getting across the finish line. Do you have a moment?" Lawrence sounded very confident as he spoke; he was quick and to the point.

"Of course. How can I help?"

We spoke for nearly an hour while I sat parked on the shoulder of the road. He explained the history of the company, who was involved, and where it was headed. I don't remember if he ever placed an actual value on the company, but it sounded like it was poised to be in the billions.

Lawrence went on to explain that he needed my help for a thirty-day project to set up a formal Investor Relations department. He needed someone to develop a process for handling investor inquiries, as all investor calls were currently being routed to a voicemail box. His Vice President was doing her best to return the calls as they came in, but this wouldn't suffice for the new company after the offering.

He also needed all the investor records verified and cleaned up. The investor database was a mess. Lawrence was suspicious that the records indicated some of the investors owned more shares than they actually did, so it would be our job to go through every record and verify that we had proof of payment. If we didn't, we were to contact the investor and ask them for a copy of the cleared check. We then adjusted the records accordingly.

There were thousands of records.

"Can you help me secure an office, set up the necessary systems, and hire the personnel to handle the volume of inquiries and records management?" he asked.

"I know just what to do and who to call," I declared. "When do you want to start?"

"Yesterday!" he cried.

Lawrence, like Wes, was excited; he spoke so rapidly that I had to ask him to repeat himself several times throughout the conversation.

He offered me a $15,000 consulting fee for the month. Then he said that once we crossed the "finish line" – a phrase I later discovered he would use often to describe the imminent IPO – I was to be on-call at half that rate for another 90 days.

The thirty days turned in to fifteen months at the same rate of pay, and that turned into thirty-three months of incarceration. I certainly never saw *that* coming.

By the time we were done talking, I could not refuse his offer. I agreed to set up the investor relations department, and felt like I was levitating on the ceiling of the car with excitement!

A Job Offer!

"Rachel, I can't wait to tell you what just happened!" I was nearly shouting with excitement as I burst through the front door.

"What?" she asked, eager to hear my news while preparing a meal at the stove.

I proceeded to tell her about the phone call and the offer, but something was wrong. As I described the details, her countenance fell. Her excitement waned by the minute. I was perplexed, but I kept sharing.

Once I finished, all she could say was, "Interesting."

"Interesting? Just interesting?" I muttered, confused by her lack of enthusiasm.

"I don't think you should do this," she said suddenly. "I really think you should stay focused on opening the real estate office."

"What?" I said, completely dumbfounded. *Did she not hear what I just said? Fifteen thousand dollars!*

"This is only a thirty-day project," I protested. "I can put the real estate office on hold for a bit. And we could really use that money right now, while we're waiting for the stock to go public." I started getting frustrated. "What possible reason is there for me not to take this opportunity?"

"I really don't know," Rachel admitted, undeterred. "I can't put my finger on it, but I just *feel* like it's not a good idea."

"But, Rach," I pushed, "we lost our portfolio, my job and our savings to survive this long. We need the money. It could be *months* before I close any real estate commissions. Besides," I added, "isn't this an answer to prayer?"

We *had* exhausted our savings. I wasn't sure how we were going to pay all of our bills the following month, so the two of us had prayed for a miracle.

"Rach, we *just* prayed for a financial miracle. Then, a few days later, I get this offer from Lawrence. Don't you think that's the miracle we asked for?"

"I can't explain it, Kevin," she repeated, "but I just don't have a good feeling about you working with this guy, and getting distracted from your original vision."

"Well, I disagree," I said, running out of steam, but stubborn nonetheless. "And I've already committed to the project. I'll be done in 30 days and back on track with the real estate company. Everything will be fine. You'll see."

Rachel couldn't come up with any rational explanation for her feeling; she was just being intuitive in the moment.

Of course, she was completely right. And boy, was I wrong.

THE JOB

The next day I set out to find an office. My search turned up a turnkey suite in a skyrise in downtown Bellevue, Washington. It would take a week to prepare the space with a secure computer network and equip the door with a hand-scanner keyless entry.

Each computer would be equipped with a thumbprint scanner for logging in. The server had three removable hard drives, and at the end of each day, I would take one drive home and place it in a safe; another team member would do the same. Both drives had to be reinserted into the machine in the morning for the data to be accessible.

In order to access the office suite, each team member would enter a security code and place their full hand on a handprint scanner. If verified, the door would unlock.

I was all very Jason Bourne; it seemed to me that Lawrence was a bit paranoid about these security measures. After all, this was supposed to be the Investor Relations department, not a vault where top-secret formulas were secured. He claimed we had serious competition that would try to access the company records.

Inside the suite was a main room where six cubicles were set up, each with a computer and phone. Adjoining that room was another room, which became my office.

The whole suite was rather sterile, with the exception of a few items of personal memorabilia on the desks. Six others worked with me here, focused exclusively on investors.

We had dozens of Banker's Boxes delivered, each containing hard copies of the investment paperwork. Each investor file included a document with the investment details, and copies of the checks they wrote to buy their stock. Lots of the investors made multiple purchases at different times, and each purchase was in a different file. The files were not in any logical or alphabetical order.

The team members would each grab a handful of files, then search the database for matching records. If everything was correct, the documents would then be scanned and electronically linked with their record. After the document was successfully scanned, the hard file was placed in a different box, earmarked to be professionally shredded. Lawrence did not want any paper records that might easily be copied, misplaced or obtained by the competition.

When there was a discrepancy, the team member would contact the investor and ask for copies of their canceled checks. Of course, most investors would readily comply. After all, they didn't want their portfolio to be shortchanged. Unfortunately, more than a reasonable number of investors protested providing proof of purchase. It turned out that most of the protesters were unwilling or unable to provide proof of their purchase; we adjusted their records accordingly, much to their chagrin.

In addition to our internal work and outbound phone calls, our phones were ringing off the hooks with calls from investors – some were returning our calls, but many just wanted an update on the imminent IPO. At least once each day we would have a disgruntled investor asking for their money back. These were usually the ones who purchased stock in the early years and were getting tired of waiting for Lawrence to take the company public, but Lawrence had a no refund policy. If an investor pushed his buttons enough, he would instruct the treasurer to issue the refund, but that was rare.

One of our instructions was to remove any record of commissions paid to the salespeople. Lawrence explained that the investor files and the commissions paid needed to be completely separate for the audit. Unfortunately, the majority of the paper copies had handwritten notes showing which salesperson sold the stock, and how much they were paid. The typical commission was ten percent, but there were a few paid at fifteen percent. Lawrence was a little perturbed that the commission amounts had been handwritten on the investor paperwork, and told us to white-out the handwritten notes, then scan the documents into the computers. The original documents would later be shredded, once all the records were accurate.

This is the moment something started to really bother me. I wasn't sure if it was the idea that we were "cleaning up" the paperwork in preparation for the final audit, or unlicensed salespeople earning commissions. Maybe it was both.

I do remember being too intimidated by Lawrence to question him about it. So, I decided to bring it up with Conrad.

THE FINDER'S FEE

The next day Conrad stopped by to check on our progress. I used this opportunity to ask him how they were able to justify paying commissions for stock sales to any salesperson who did not have a securities license. Conrad explained that the company was allowed to pay finder's fees to people *introducing* an investor. In sales, this is also known as a "bird dog" or "referral" fee paid to a third party. I understood referral fees from my own sales background, so it made sense.

That's when I discovered that Wes, my friend from church, was one of the recipients of these 'finder's' fees.

Apparently, his offer to me was not quite as altruistic as it appeared, I thought. *There was more than a little profit motive involved.*

Up until this point, I'd referred numerous friends and family to the company. This was merely out of my zeal for the opportunity, and most of them purchased stock. I learned then that Wes had earned a healthy amount of money on *all* of *my* referrals.

After confirming the fact with Conrad, I asked if I could start collecting my own finder's fees for the referrals I was providing, and he agreed. I would start collecting ten percent on each of my referrals from that point on.

Ironically, I never mentioned this fact to *my* family and friends, either. What a hypocrite! Thankfully, the majority of my friends and all of my family members have since forgiven my misguided advice.

I continued to spread the exciting short-term investment opportunity to the people I knew and cared about. This time, of course, with even more zeal – knowing I would be profiting from referrals.

Getting paid for referrals didn't change the heart-felt belief in the company or investment opportunity. Or did it?

INCENTIVE-CAUSED BLIND SPOT

Looking back, I now realize I was influenced by what Charles Munger calls the Incentive-caused bias. He explains, "It's human nature to veer toward behavior that benefits you, while simultaneously believing that you're serving the greater good."[21]

Finding out about the finder's fee helped me rationalize my initial concern about those handwritten "commission" notes that we would be cleaning up. I figured the person referring the investor had a vested interest in making sure their "finder's fee" was documented in the file; that's how they got paid. Sure, the company could probably have had a better system for this, but at least it made sense.

---

[21] On the psychology of human misjudgment. Charles T. Munger, 1985

The concern about the licensing was also no longer a problem. Being a recipient of the finder's fees assuaged my earlier concerns about whether or not a securities license was really necessary. I accepted Conrad's explanation, and happily rationalized that Lawrence would certainly not authorize a practice that would jeopardize the public offering.

I had no idea what I was in for next.

> *Blind Spot Challenge: What decisions are you making that are influenced by the Incentive-caused Blind Spot?*

BUSINESS AS USUAL

Everyone on the IR team worked feverishly to verify each investment, clean the paperwork, scan the documents, field investor calls and questions, and prepare for the "final audit" – a term Lawrence threw at us frequently, inferring that we were close to the "finish line."

I can't remember ever hearing Lawrence use the technical term "Initial Public Offering" or "IPO." I don't believe he ever said "reverse-merger" or even "public offering." He didn't need to; he was a master of inference. He used words like "final audit," which we all accepted (without any real confirmation) as the last step in the process of going public. He used words like "finish line," supposedly referring to a time when the company would finally be a public company listed on the NASDAQ. He spoke frequently about the auditing and legal teams, and how they were working around the clock to "get things done." When asked specifically about the S-1 filing (the SEC paperwork for an IPO), his response was "the paperwork is the Holy Grail. Everyone wants to see the paperwork. But only a few people are allowed."

From that point on, we all spoke and even dreamed of this "Holy Grail." It was the rabbit we all chased, running endlessly on Lawrence's track.

We worked long days, and sometimes even Saturdays, pushing hard to meet his deadlines to cross that allusive *finish line.*

THE FINISH LINE

Unfortunately, the finish line kept moving. Lawrence had us pushing hard for a Fall 2000 "finish line," but he never gave us a specific date. All he said was that he hoped to be done before the November 2000 Presidential election.

As the election drew near, our phones were lighting up with excited investors wanting to know if we were on track for the IPO. And all any of us could say was, "As far as we've been told, we're on track."

But as you might guess, the election came and went – and no IPO. To say we were disappointed is an understatement. We had to say something. So, with several of my team members listening, I called Lawrence and asked him what happened.

"Our board decided it would not be a good move to make the announcement right now, with all the election turmoil going on. We're pushing things back to the first of the year. But don't worry; the markets will be better prepared for us in a few months, so we can maximize our launch." Lawrence explained everything in a cryptic sort of way, never giving too many details.

His explanation did not make any of us in IR happy, but our Confirmation Bias allowed us to accept what he said. We had no reason to suspect he was lying. We were all heavily invested in the company, fixated on the increasing values of our stock. We *wanted* to believe what he said, so we *did*. His explanation satisfied us just enough to keep the faith.

Stuart, one member of the IR team, was less happy than the rest of us. He didn't lose his faith in the company, but he definitely suffered; he and his wife had just bought and moved into a very large, new house. They'd based that decision solely on the windfall they thought they'd receive from the IPO!

The house was double what they had been living in – and so was the payment. According to Stuart, they convinced the builder to allow them to move in early on a rental basis with the expectation that they would have the money to close escrow as soon as the IPO took place.

Stuart had a lot of explaining to do.

After word of the delay quickly made its way through the investor community the phones rang off the hook. We began to learn that there were a *lot* of people just like Stuart, who'd made commitments based on the announcement of the imminent IPO. Now they were scrambling to unwind financial commitments they couldn't possibly keep.

A couple investors requested their money back, but the treasurer denied those requests. For the most part, the rest of the investors just accepted the news and patiently waited for the next scheduled IPO after the holidays.

Everyone was living on hope.

Cope When You Have Hope

There is a saying I think of often: *"You can cope when you have hope."* Lawrence was a master at feeding hope to the investor community. He kept everyone focused on crossing the "finish line," even when the finish line was pushed back again and again.

I spoke with investors every day. Most of them had grandiose visions of how they were going to spend their newfound wealth. A common theme was a desire to fund their local libraries, or build shelters for the homeless; many dreamed of retiring from their mundane jobs to volunteer at orphanages or soup kitchens. The list of causes and humanitarian ideas was extensive; it almost seemed too good to be true. I grew a little cynical, and started questioning their motives by asking what they planned to do *personally* with the money. That's when the other side of the stories came to light: They would buy new homes, of course, as well as new cars, new clothes, and many planned to travel the world. Hidden under the shroud of generosity was greed.

"Wait!" I can hear you protesting now. "What's wrong with spending some of the profits on upgrading your lifestyle a little bit, huh?"

What, indeed.

THE LITTLE GUY

Lawrence was proud of the fact that he was building an empire that would benefit the average person, the "little guy," as he often referred to the investors.

Most of the investors were typical middle-class Americans. Many of them invested in the company from their retirement accounts. Some increased the mortgages on their homes to invest. Others scraped together every last nickel on the promise that they would be able to cash in their stock in just a few months, and surely become wealthy beyond their wildest dreams. Suddenly everyone developed a sense of social responsibility. I'm sure some of these people were sincerely interested in using their wealth for others, but most were just self-deceived.

If you find yourself focused on becoming wealthy, you might have an undetected greed issue. But, if you also find yourself justifying those thoughts with all the good you plan to do with the money, you might be impacted by the Materialism Blind Spot.

Are you constantly dreaming of winning the lottery? Are you hoping a long-lost wealthy uncle will show up and give you a substantial gift? Are you working tirelessly to strike it rich with your business ventures? Are you so driven to climb the corporate ladder that the rest of your family and health is suffering? These might be indicators of a greed issue.

Have you ever justified your long hours at work by saying you're doing it to provide for your family? Though it might sound altruistic, it could be the Materialism Blind Spot. Of course, altruism itself is not a bad thing. But when it becomes a blind spot that covers up an ulterior motive or character deficiency, that's when you need change your thinking.

Take some time right now and ask yourself those questions. Honestly evaluate the answers. You might not like what you find. But if you don't identify these blind spots, you could be on a collision course with catastrophe.

> *Blind Spot Challenge: What habit, motives, or character deficiencies might you be covering up with altruistic ideas?*

KERNELS OF TRUTH BLIND SPOT

When I first invested in the company, I was told that numerous sports celebrities were involved. I had no proof. But, since

Wes said it, I assumed he was telling the truth.

Then I found the document. One of the investors called the IR department to warn us: we had a leak.

"Kevin, this is John. I thought you should know that someone in the company is leaking information that looks like it should be confidential."

"What do you mean?" I asked, puzzled.

"What's your fax number? I'll send it over right now."

I waited by the machine. A couple of minutes later, I received the document. I was stunned.

"John, this is incredible," I said, calling him back. "Thank you for bringing this to my attention. I'll let Lawrence know right away!" I knew I had to inform Lawrence about this now; someone had to put a stop to it.

"But – is it true?" he cried, determined not to let me off the phone.

"I have no idea, John," I explained. "I've heard from a good source that these people are in fact part of the company. But Lawrence has never confirmed or denied it."

The document looked very official. It listed the board of directors, officers and other key individuals involved in the company, and included celebrities like John Elway, Kareem Abdul-Jabbar, Shaquille O'Neal, and Olympic runner Michael Johnson. Another name that wasn't as well known, but nonetheless extremely important, was Dr. Charles J. Dillman, the former head of the Medical Commission of the International Olympic committee. He was the incoming CEO, and was scheduled to replace Lawrence, who would then become Chairman of the Board.

It was rumored that Shaq had paid $100,000 to pre-purchase a license to open up his own Znetix location. However, in all likelihood, it was probably the other way around. Based on a lawsuit[22] filed by investors a couple of years later, it's more likely that Lawrence actually paid some of these people for their endorsements, and then just used their names to further his scheme.

When questioned about the list, Lawrence was always irate that it was in the open. He never actually affirmed or denied the veracity of the document, he just let us assume what we wanted to believe. With our Confirmation Bias hard at work, the list was one more item of proof that we were on the right track.

It got better, for our confirmation biases, at least. I would soon discover that at least some of the names on the list were in fact affiliated with the company.

Lawrence paid for several of his key team members, including me, to fly to Los Angeles for a celebration party sponsored by Znetix, in honor of Shaquille O'Neal.

At the airport, two limousine drivers stood near baggage claim holding nameplates. They were waiting to take us to the Four Seasons Hotel. After checking in and freshening up, we piled back into the limos, which drove us to the party.

We arrived a few minutes later and pulled up to a somewhat non-descript, white building. As we walked through a gazebo-like entrance into a large yard, there were dozens of

---

[22] Cook, John (2003, Feb 3). *Znetix lawsuit names sports figures*. Retrieved from http://www.seattlepi.com/business/article/Znetix-lawsuit-names-sports-figures-1106708.php

people milling around with drinks. On the side of the building was a large Znetix banner. Parked by the entrance was a new high-performance motorcycle, painted with the green and white company colors and our logo on the gas tank.

The party started the minute we walked through the doors. The music was loud, the hallways and rooms were dimly lit, and people were everywhere.

We made our way through the crowd, looking for the bar. As we walked down a long passageway towards what looked like the dance floor, Shaquille O'Neal and Kobe Bryant actually walked right past us. Shaq was even wearing a Znetix baseball cap. We were ecstatic; I think we were more excited about the fact that he was wearing a company hat than anything else. Needless to say, our concerns about the list were immediately allayed.

Bodyguards and beautiful women surrounded the two celebrities, who mostly kept to themselves. Apparently, there was a separate party going on in one of the back rooms. Shaq and Kobe entered through a door guarded by a well-dressed bouncer. Only a select few were allowed to enter, and that didn't include us.

The next day we flew home. What a trip; we were so excited to see firsthand that the names on the list were real.

KEEPING UP THE FAÇADE

Lawrence spent millions to keep up the façade.

He paid for billboards on the metro buses driving throughout the Los Angeles area. He had billboards in Safeco field, where the Seattle Mariners play. He even owned a suite at the ballpark, and frequently invited investors and staff to watch games from his suite.

When it came to putting on a show, Lawrence was the best. I learned he was masterful at what the FBI called "Kernels of truth, stuffed with a lie."

These kernels meant that he spent money lavishly if it would encourage the fundraisers to continue to sell stock, and keep the investors patient and excited about the future. We discovered much later that he was also spending an enormous amount of money on himself. He secretly purchased a $330,000 diamond ring for his fiancé using investor funds. He purchased several homes, including a house and land in Hawaii. He owned motorhomes, Hummers, luxury import cars, motorcycles and boats.[23] How could we doubt him when he so clearly had the wealth he told us we would soon receive?

They were kernels.

You can be affected by the Kernels of Truth Blind Spot when you accept facts at face value, without digging deeper to verify the truth. We easily do this as consumers, especially in the grocery aisles. You grab an item off the shelf, assuming it meets your personal nutritional requirements based on the front label – which was designed by expert marketers to appeal to your *desires*, not to meet any nutritional need. They're trying to make a sale. If you actually read the small print, you might see that the number one ingredient is high-fructose corn syrup.

But this doesn't happen just with food. Perhaps most detrimentally, you do this in your research, as well. Whether we are studying a subject for personal edification, performing an audit, or compiling data to place in a report for the boss, very rarely do we really verify the sources of our information and dig deep enough to find multiple perspectives and really understand the whole picture.

---

[23] Cook, John (2002, Aug 26). *Znetix auction brings in about $1.5 million*. Retrieved from http://www.seattlepi.com/business/article/Znetix-auction-brings-in-about-1-5-million-1094503.php

For a simple example of how to become more cognizant of this blind spot, the next time you are about to buy a food product, turn it over and read the label. Do you know what all the ingredients are? Are you comfortable the product meets your standards, as the front label would have you believe?

When researching, ask yourself if you are satisfied that you have obtained enough perspectives and verified the veracity of your sources. Don't just trust one article – dig for opposing viewpoints, and make an informed decision.

Action Tip: Dig deeper to verify the source before you accept something as absolutely true.

PRESS RELEASES

Lawrence would occasionally have IR send out press releases to investors about the purchase of other companies. More kernels.

On one such occasion, he said his company purchased Barnhart Labs to acquire their state-of-the-art technology. As he was describing the acquisition, something he said gave me an uncomfortable feeling. I can't remember exactly if it was something he said, or something he didn't say. But it was enough to push me to contact Barnhart Labs myself to validate the story.

I told the person who answered the phone that I was the head of Investor Relations and worked for Lawrence. They put me right through to Mr. Barnhart.

He sounded a bit exasperated as he explained that I was one of numerous calls they'd received in the last 24 hours from our investors. It seems I was not the only one who wanted to verify this story.

"Listen, Mr. Lawrence and I are in discussions under NDA (a non-disclosure agreement)," Barnhart explained. "All I can tell you is that he gave us a large deposit, and we are discussing the future of our company."

That was all I needed to hear. Once again, he confirmed what we wanted to believe. The company was growing with these acquisitions in preparation for a significant public offering.

I relayed my Barnhart conversation to any investor who asked. It seemed not just to quell their concerns, but in fact acted as a shot of adrenaline to their hope. The more press releases – especially verified ones – the more excited the investor community became, and the more money the company raised. Everyone was spreading the news to friends and family, including me.

My parents and sisters invested. My best friend and many close friends invested. My father-in-law invested. I was contacting everyone in my sphere of influence. All the while my personal stock portfolio was also growing, because I often accepted commissions in stock instead of cash. Lawrence would also give out stock, and sometimes cash, as bonuses for hard work or meeting deadlines.

At the pinnacle of the fifteen months with the company, I believed my stock portfolio would be worth well over two million dollars when the company finally went public.

BACK IN THE GAME

I felt like I was back in the game! The money I lost in the dot com bubble was soon to be replaced.

The opportunity seemed even more significant from an ego standpoint. When I sold my previous company to Homeseekers.com and became the President of its broker division, I felt like I had arrived; I felt like a huge success.

But, now that I was sitting on such a healthy portfolio and working directly for the CEO of what would become a multi-billion dollar IPO, my ego went through the roof. My head was so large that I needed a double-door to get into my office. It was disgusting, actually, and I'm embarrassed to admit it.

One day Stuart asked if he could speak with me in the conference room. I complied with great curiosity.

"Kev," he said, "I love you at church. I love you outside of church. But, here in the office... you're a jerk!"

I was stunned. I could hardly believe this guy could call his own boss into the conference room and call me a jerk! I was sorely tempted to fire him on the spot.

Thankfully, I had the sense to ponder his words carefully before I responded. I'd like to say that I agreed with him and humbly tried to learn from the experience, but I didn't go quite that far.

Instead, I diplomatically explained that I was under a lot of pressure from Lawrence, and I needed to be tough in order to meet deadlines. I basically justified my behavior, rather than even vaguely considering what he had to say.

He probably didn't like my answer. But he accepted it, and we went back to work.

It took time in prison to stop and reflect on *why* I was such a jerk. That's when I knew I needed to change.

A LIFE OF QUIET DESPERATION

As I was climbing the ladder of success, secretly I lived a life of quiet desperation.

Life was so fast and furious that I never had enough time to breath and reflect. I secretly wished I could just escape to a cabin deep in the woods, away from people and technology. I thought if I could just get six months of solitude, I could figure out who I was and where I was going.

Well, I got my wish. It just wasn't 6 months in a cabin. It was 33 months in a federal prison, with 503 roommates, and constant noise.

Hopefully you won't have to go to prison to make the changes you need to make in your own life.

Action Tip: Are you feeling out of balance? Slow down, be intentional and be content.

THE LEADERSHIP CONUNDRUM

What I learned from that moment with Stuart was that I had lost sight of what authentic leadership really looks like. I had a leadership conundrum and didn't even realize it. I was so driven to get all the tasks completed and be ready for the IPO that I completely overlooked the people factor. It didn't even dawn on me that I was not investing in my team. In fact, I was being disrespectful and had little regard for their well-being as I pushed them hard to complete time-constrained projects.

Have you ever noticed how people use the terms "leadership" and "management" interchangeably? This is one of the colloquial *faux pas* of our time. Truth is, "leadership" and "management" mean completely different things.

In the words of Rear Admiral Grace Murray Hopper, "You manage things, you lead people."[24] Yet, in the frenzy of meeting deadlines and budgets, you quickly get wrapped up in the management minutia. You start managing people as if they are just tools in your process. As you can probably imagine, people generally don't like to be managed, especially on a micro level.

Ultimately, a leader's job is to get results. But part of those results depends on developing and influencing people. In order to do that, a leader must know and *understand* her people. And even that is difficult to do if that leader doesn't fully understand herself.

A leader's greatest personal challenge is to constantly be a student of human behavior. Self-awareness and awareness of others are the keys to authentic leadership.

"When the 75 members of the Stanford Graduate School of Business's Advisory Council were asked to recommend the most important capability for leaders to develop, their answer was nearly unanimous: self-awareness. Yet many leaders, especially early in their careers, are trying so hard to establish themselves in the world that they leave little time for self-exploration."[25]

The problem with self-awareness is too many of us are too busy to take the necessary time to reflect. We do not see the value in investing time and resources into personal growth, or 'soft-skills' training. We are too distracted to create a habit of

---

[24] Schieber, Philip (from the OCLC Newsletter, March /April 1987, No. 167). *The wit and wisdom of Grace Hopper.* Retrieved from http://www.cs.yale.edu/homes/tap/Files/hopper-wit.html
[25] George, Sims, McLean, Mayer, (Feb 2007 issue). Harvard Business Review, *Discovering Your Authentic Leadership*

reading personal and professional growth books or going to workshops (Of course, I'm talking about all those other leaders, not you! You made the wise choice to set aside the time to read this book. Kudos to you!).

The Leadership Conundrum is a blind spot that hinders your effectiveness and influence. Leadership expert Jeff Kauflin, in his Forbes article on self-awareness, sums it up nicely: "Self-awareness is critical for career success. People who are more self-aware tend to perform better at work, get more promotions, and lead more effectively. Companies with more self-aware professionals have shown stronger financial performance."[26]

Sadly, according to organizational psychologist Tasha Eurich, "Ninety-five percent of people think they're self-aware, but only 10-15% truly are."[27] I was one of the many who was not self-aware. Prison was a strong wakeup call.

Whenever we facilitate our transformational leadership workshops, we always ask the audience for a show of hands to see who has completed a DISC or similar personality profile assessment. The response is less than twenty percent. I'm always amazed. On top of that, the majority of the twenty percent admit to not actually using the information they learned to become better leaders.

Personality and performance assessments are not just theories to have fun with in seminars. The good ones are backed by extensive research and proven to be accurate over decades of field study.

---

[26] Kauflin, Jeff (2017, May 10). *Only 15% of people are self-aware - - here's how to change.* Retrieved from
https://www.forbes.com/sites/jeffkauflin/2017/05/10/only-15-of-people-are-self-aware-heres-how-to-change
[27] Ibid.

SCIENCE OF DISC PERSONALITY STYLES

The science of DISC personality temperaments has been around for millennia, but it was the Greek physician Hippocrates (460–370 BC) who developed it into a medical theory. He believed certain human moods, emotions and behaviors were caused by an excess or lack of body fluids (called "humors"): blood, yellow bile, black bile, and phlegm.[28]

In 1928, when American psychologist and lawyer William Moulton "Charles" Marston published his book, *Emotions of Normal People,* he laid the foundation for the future of DISC assessments and their place in the corporate world. Though he developed the original DISC model and theory, Marston did not create an actual assessment tool. It was the prominent psychologist and professor John Geier, who developed the first DISC Personality Profile System in the 1970's.

Since then, many DISC assessment tools have been developed; a few of them are tried and true. To be sure you are using the original DISC tool, look for the lower case "i" (DiSC®) and the registered trademark after the "C" owned by Everything DiSC®, a Wiley Brand.

Our company uses the original DiSC® and several other assessment tools to help individuals, teams and organizations uncover the blind spots that affect their behavior and decision-making and develop stronger, more cohesive and inclusive cultures. We also simplified the discovery process for our clients by developing our own Blind Spot Assessment tool. A complimentary assessment is available to you using the information on page 205 in this book.

To avoid the Leadership Conundrum, you must become more cognizant to differentiate how you manage systems from

---

[28] Retrieved from https://en.wikipedia.org/wiki/Four_temperaments

how you lead your people.

> *Blind Spot Challenge: What are you doing to improve as a leader? And, what are you doing to develop the leadership skills of those around you?*

CONTINUED DELAYS

The entire time I was with HMC, Lawrence continued to delay the IPO for one reason or another. For instance, he delayed the IPO because of the famous "hanging chads" 2000 presidential election, saying the market was distracted. There was always an excuse, and for some reason, the excuse always made sense to us.

The investors became increasingly frustrated and impatient. The IR team was growing weary of the long hours and difficult phone calls. Since each of us on the IR team was a shareholder as well, we were also getting impatient.

Nothing could have prepared us for what happened next.

CHAPTER FOUR:

HANGING ON TO HOPE

CEASE AND DESIST

On April 9, 2001, the state of Washington issued a cease-and-desist order instructing the company to quit selling stock. The decree was published in the local newspapers and the word traveled coast to coast rapidly through the investor community. The IR phones were ringing so constantly we had to shut them off so we could figure out what was going on.

To say that we were freaked out would be an understatement. We were confused, angry, and deeply discouraged. We could not wrap our minds around what this could mean.

It didn't sound good, that was for sure.

I grabbed Jackson, who was a former stockbroker Lawrence hired as a fundraiser, and Wes, and brought them into my office where we immediately called Lawrence. Surely, he'd have some answers, right?

It went to voicemail.

"Hey Lawrence, this is Kevin. Everyone is freaking out over here in IR. Please – call me back ASAP! We need help understanding what the hell is going on!"

The three of us could hardly speak. We stood there, staring at the phone in shock, until we finally exchanged a frightened glance. I could tell by their expressions we were all wondering the same thing: *What the heck did we get ourselves into?*

Just a couple of minutes later, my phone rang.

"Kevin? This is Lawrence. I need you guys all to settle down. Take a deep breath." I put the phone on speaker so the others could be a part of the conversation.

"Listen," Lawrence continued, surprisingly calm. "You know that I built this company for the little guy. It's always been my passion to build this company so everyone is a winner. Right? Well, that's what I've done, and now the regulators want to bust my chops over it.

"They say I've sold too much stock to people who are not qualified to buy stock in a private company," he continued. "Most of our investors are ordinary folks like you guys, just trying to get ahead. It sounds like I am going to get slapped with some healthy fines, and they want me to stop allowing any other investors to join us in our quest." He paused, just long enough for me to barge in to his diatribe.

"So," I jumped in, "what does that mean for the company? What does that mean for all of our investors? What are we supposed to tell them?"

"Tell them nothing has changed," he said, trying to alleviate our concerns. "We are still moving forward. We will cross the finish line. My legal team is working on a strategy that will make everyone happy. In the meantime, the State wants us to do a rescission offering."

"What does *that* mean?" I snapped.

"Kevin, I need you to gain your composure," Lawrence insisted. "People respect you; I can't have you fall apart on me. The investors look to you and your team for solace. Don't let me down. Okay?"

"I don't want to let you down," I said, with a calmer voice.

"But I need to understand what's going on, and how on earth you think this won't affect the public offering."

"Listen, Kevin, it's simple. A company is only allowed to have up to 35 unaccredited investors. We have thousands. I've crossed the line and violated some securities rules. Now, in order to make it good again, we need to send every investor a prospectus that shows the risk of their investment. They will then have the option of *rescinding* their purchase and requesting a full refund along with a mandatory eight percent interest. Or, they can sign the prospectus and agree to hold their stock in full support of the company moving forward. Make sense?" He barely took a breath before continuing.

"Once the rescission offering is completed and I'm slapped with the fines, we'll be free to finish the project. Okay?" Finally, he paused and waited for my response.

"That sounds simple enough," I said, still feeling nervous about the whole thing. "But what happens if too many investors want their money back and you end up broke?"

Wes jumped into the conversation. "Lawrence, this is Wes. Didn't you know you were over the legal limits on the number of investors?"

"Yes!" Lawrence admitted, shocking us all. "My attorneys warned me about this months ago. But we all decided the benefits of winning this race outweighed the potential amount of the fines that might be imposed. I would do it all over again if that's what it takes to make our investors rich! Everyone is going to have their dreams come true very soon. If we let the regulators win, everyone else loses. Got it?"

"Yeah, that makes sense," Wes said, trying to find his own solace in the chaos. "I just wish you would have warned us."

Jackson took his opportunity to speak up, "Lawrence, this is Jackson. As you know, I'm one of the guys in the field helping you raise the funds. You're always telling us we need more money for the audit and legal teams, as well as operations. So where is this money for the rescission offering going to come from? I have to believe we'll have a lot of investors bail after they hear the news."

"Great question, and a long answer. I have to run into this meeting with my lawyers and the state. I'll get back to you with the answer later. Bye."

And with that, he hung up.

We looked at each other again, eyebrows raised. We still didn't feel great about this, but Jackson put us at ease for the moment. As a former licensed stockbroker, he explained that he'd heard of these rescission offerings, and they are in fact as Lawrence explained them. Jackson's only concern was in actually having the money to back the offer in the event of a refund request.

I did my best to explain the situation to the rest of the IR team, and we fielded calls for the next few hours.

Then my phone rang. It was Lawrence. Again.

THE CALL CENTER

"Hey Kevin it's Lawrence." He spoke so quickly; the words were nearly unintelligible – like a tech support rep who answers and speaks so fast you forget which company you called in the first place.

"Hey! What's up?" I wondered if he was calling back to answer Jackson's question.

"Listen, the state will not let us do the rescission offering unless we can guarantee that we will have the funds to pay back the investors who opt out. So, I need you to contact every investor immediately to get a pulse on how much money we are going to need. Can you do that?" He asked so abruptly, it seemed as if he thought I'd already have an answer.

"Uh, well, hmm," I said buying some time, "let me think… we'll need to put together a telephone room, and bring in a couple dozen people to make the outbound calls. Are you okay with spending the money?"

"Yeah. We don't have a choice. Hire a bunch of temps, give them scripts and monitor the results. I need to get a read on how many people might bail on us once they have the chance. Figure it out, then call me later." And he hung up.

I updated the team and asked everyone to think of anyone they knew in the investor community who might be available for two or three days of calls. I figured the best thing we could do for the IR department was to hire investors as temps if possible; maybe, if they knew for themselves what was happening, our phones wouldn't ring as much.

I checked with the landlord who allowed us to rent a small training room for the week and equip it with tables, chairs and twenty-five telephones.

We called our list of investors and everyone jumped at the opportunity to make the calls to the rest of the community. Some of the investor volunteers were retired. Others took time off from their jobs. Some were real estate agents or other self-employed individuals who controlled their own work schedule. Regardless of their occupation, they were all excited to become "insiders," even if just for a moment. They wanted to know firsthand what was happening with their investment and where the company was heading, and helping us was a simple enough strategy. That made it easy to find a group of twenty-five people to make the calls from morning until night.

Within a week we had reached almost all of the 5,000 investors, and tallied their answers. The telephone survey went something like this:

> "Hi Investor (insert their name), this is (insert your name) calling from the HMC/Znetix offices. I need to ask you a couple quick questions about your investment with the company. Is that okay?

> "Thank you! As you know, the State of Washington is requiring us to send you a new prospectus detailing the high risk involved with your investment. You will have one of two options when you receive it. You will be offered the opportunity to receive your full investment back along with eight percent interest. Or, you can sign the waiver and keep your investment in the company as we push hard to reach our goals of going public.

> "Do you think at this point you would be inclined to request a refund or to keep your stock in the company?"

Most of the investors we spoke with agreed to the survey. And less than two percent of them said they would request a refund! We were elated; it was an amazing relief that the vast majority of the investor community still believed in the company and wanted to stand with us.

It didn't really seem odd to us that so many investors wanted to stay even after knowing about the cease and desist order. Though some vocalized frustrations, most people were still enamored with the idea of receiving large returns on their investments. They were also big believers in Lawrence, regardless of what the media reported. It was as if he had a spell over five thousand people. Under different circumstances, he might have rivaled the magic of the famed illusionist David Copperfield.

THE WHITE KNIGHT

"Kevin, that's great!" Lawrence was, like us, extremely relieved at the report, and of course had specific instructions for how to proceed. "It sounds like we will only need two to three million dollars to cover any refund requests. That's totally doable. I really didn't expect much more than that. This company was built on the little guy; I knew they'd support us through this crap.

"Kevin," he went on, "according to the state, we need a white knight to back and fund the rescission. Basically, that means we need a separate investment company that's willing to put up the funds. It can't have anything to do with me."

I hesitated, unsure what he was getting at. "This is a great opportunity," he pressed, "for a few of our more sophisticated investors to own a larger share of the company."

He hesitated, and I was still perplexed. "I'm not sure what you mean."

"It's simple, Kevin. Find a boutique law firm in Bellevue. Tell them the situation. Ask them to set up an LLC. Pick a name for it, any name, it doesn't matter. Once the LLC is set up, you need to hire a manager. Do you know anyone who is qualified to lead an investment company?"

"As a matter of fact, I do," I said, happy to have something to offer. "My good friend George doesn't have an investment background, but he has a PhD, and three other degrees, and taught business management at a university. He's qualified to be the managing partner." George was a good friend, and I was excited that I might be able to offer him such a great opportunity. After all this stress, I was looking for a silver lining.

"Perfect! Once the LLC is ready, and George is on board, go through our database and contact the top 100 investors. Tell them to call George if they want to make history and join forces to become the white knight. They will collectively be the largest single shareholder of the new company. Understand?"

I didn't exactly understand. It took a while to process, but I didn't want to say that.

"Got it!" I said instead. "I'll call you when it's all set. Oh, who is paying the legal fees?"

"Call Conrad," he said, which was exactly as I expected. "He'll cut a cashier's check for whatever retainer they require."

Then he hung up without saying goodbye – a practice that was becoming his norm.

I told Jackson and Wes everything I had just learned, and since Jackson had some experience in the matter, he filled us in on the details. The biggest thing we learned from Jackson was that this rescission offering was good news. It was a remedy for the violations and would sort of cover over Lawrence's sins; it would allow the company to move forward. Jackson was excited, and we were excited that he was excited.

But something still bothered me.

I couldn't put my finger on it. After all, everything made sense after Lawrence and Jackson explained it. Maybe I was just nervous because I was venturing into unfamiliar territory? I wasn't sure; I wanted to check it out a little more before I contacted a law firm.

BE SKEPTICAL BUT NOT CYNICAL

This was not the first or last time I felt a need to validate what Lawrence was telling us. Although I couldn't put my finger on why, there was just something nagging me to dig deeper. So, I did. This was one of those intuitive moments. The lesson I learned, much too late, was to be more skeptical, but not cynical.

Being skeptical doesn't come easily for many of us. If your nature is to believe the best in people, or to accept information from someone at face value, then you might feel awkward about questioning what you are being told.

If you have a peacekeeper personality, you will definitely not want to ruffle anyone's feathers by appearing to challenge what they are saying. Yet it must be done.

Becoming more skeptical is healthy – until you cross the line into cynicism. Skepticism is simply requiring more insights or validity before accepting something to be true; cynicism is believing the worst about something or someone.

So, with a bit of skepticism, I called my friend Dave, who was a forensic CPA. He previously worked at the Circle K Corporation, a company of convenience stores coast to coast. Dave's job was to identify fraud at the store level. I explained to him what I was being asked to do.

"Well, Kevin, I'm not sure about any of that. I never had to deal with corporate maneuvers like that in my job. But I do know someone who will have the answers."

Dave had a friend, Jan Bittinger, who formerly worked as an attorney for the federal SEC – Securities and Exchange Commission. She currently practiced law privately in Phoenix, and Dave agreed to contact her for advice.

The next day, Dave called me back with good news. "Kevin, I spoke with Jan. She said that based on what you told me, it sounds legit. She saw this type of corporate maneuver several times during her tenure with the SEC."

"That's comforting news, Dave," I said with a sigh of relief. "Thanks for making the call!"

Of course, Jan didn't have all the facts, and neither did I. We only had kernels of truth. If Jan had all the facts, I assume she would have provided a different opinion. Lawrence had explained that the rescission offer was a remedy provided by the state to give the investors an opportunity to get their money back plus interest, since they purchased the stock without all the facts and there was no official "Reg D" filing. Though stock rescission offers are legitimate, we were only given Lawrence's version. We now know it did not necessarily absolve the company, or its officials, from potential injunctions or criminal charges for fraud.

With Jan's support of Lawrence's story, and the need for a white knight, that unsettled feeling had all but dissipated. There was just one more thing to do to completely put my mind at ease: talk to the lawyers. I needed to find a boutique law firm, just as Lawrence requested, and explain to them what I was told. "Surely," I thought, "the law firm will either support Jan's statement and Lawrence's request, or they will let me know something sounded suspect – in which case, I will have a decision to make."

THE FIRM

That afternoon, after numerous calls to very busy law firms offering the closest appointment two or more weeks out, I finally found an attorney willing to meet me as quickly as the following week. His name was John McIntyre.

When we met, I explained everything that I knew about the company, the rescission offering and the need for a white knight.

"Well, Kevin, it all makes sense. We're a boutique firm, so we have not worked with a project quite this large. But we understand the process; I'd be happy to help you guys get everything set up."

"There are no issues that you can see with what we're doing?" I asked, just to be sure we had a clear understanding.

"No, it's pretty straight-forward," John assured me. "We just need to make sure that the white knight investors are qualified, and that all the documentation is in place."

His firm wanted a $15,000 retainer to set up and represent the LLC. Conrad sent them a cashier's check.

And so, three weeks after the cease and desist was issued, George became the Managing Partner of what was then called Cascade Pointe, LLC – the white knight.

THE NEW MONEY MACHINE

George asked me about hiring staff for Cascade Pointe, as he needed an assistant to handle the paperwork for the investors.

I contacted Lawrence and asked him what he wanted to do. He said he would get back to me. A few hours later, he called back.

"Craig Vincente and his team will be flying up to Bellevue in a couple days to help get Cascade Pointe set up with the administrative procedures," he said abruptly. "Craig is one of our largest investors and huge believer in the company. We need to make sure everything is done right this time. Cascade

Pointe needs to be squeaky clean in order to satisfy the auditors and the state. Craig will be in touch with you. Got it?"

He didn't wait for an answer; he just hung up as abruptly as he'd issued his instructions. Lawrence was always abrupt on the phone. From our first conversation throughout our time together, he presented the air of being the busiest man on Earth who barely had time to squeeze in a call. I was always glad when he did, but it was also a little intimidating reporting to him. It was certainly a night and day difference from reporting to the Vice-Chairman of Homeseekers.com. Although having a conversation with Doug was much easier than with Lawrence, working with Lawrence with the anticipation of the pending IPO created a lot more adrenaline – something most entrepreneurs live for.

THE JAGUAR MAN

A couple days later, I received a call from Craig saying he was in town and heading to the Cascade Pointe office. He brought along his attorney, CPA and administrator.

I drove to the office and was greeted by George, just a few minutes before Craig drove up in a rented Jaguar. George and I looked at each other and simultaneously said, "Wow!" as if we were both wondering, "Who is this guy?"

We all met in the boardroom. Craig took charge of the meeting as if he were running Cascade Pointe. He explained that his attorney, Rob, would be handling all the paperwork, meaning the Investor Prospectus and any necessary SEC or State filings for Cascade to absorb the company. His CPA, Allen, would be managing the P&L's and making sure all the financials were in order for the final audits. His administrator, Jill, would assist George and coordinate between him and the Vincente team.

It sounded like George would be a figurehead for a well-oiled operation from a seasoned veteran, Craig. Though it was never discussed, it appeared that Craig worked for, or at least on behalf of, Lawrence. Yes, this should have been a red flag, but in the context of the moment, we didn't bat an eye. This was just another example of how we saw Lawrence as the mastermind behind a multibillion-dollar IPO, working with the "big boys" behind closed doors. According to him, he was just doing what he had to do to ensure everything moved forward in spite of the state "kicking the tires" and doing its job.

Still, poor George felt a little like he had a babysitter watching over his shoulder.

THE TOP 100

Over the next several weeks, I contacted the top 100 investors in our database and told them about Cascade Pointe. I let them know that if they were interested in being part of the white knight, they were to contact George for the details.

They did. Investment money was pouring into Cascade Pointe. Between May 2001 and December 2001 Cascade Pointe raised more than twelve million dollars.

George and I kept waiting for the rescission offering process to start. After all, that was the only reason Cascade Pointe existed and was accepting investments. At least, that's what we thought.

The rescission offering never happened.

> *Blind Spot Challenge: Be careful who you put on a pedestal. Just because someone has amassed wealth doesn't mean they should be esteemed.*

Money Transfers

Around the time that Cascade Pointe had raised its first $500,000 from two investors, Lawrence called me.

"Kevin, I need you to call George and have him issue a cashier's check to HMC for $350,000. Conrad will be over there this afternoon to pick it up. This whole white knight issue is costing us a fortune with the attorneys and auditors. And we need to cover payroll. HMC will sign a promissory note to Cascade Pointe for the bridge loan. Got it?"

All I could say was, "No problem."

It seemed odd to George and me that Lawrence was borrowing the money that we thought was reserved for the rescission offering. But, technically, the offer had not been made yet, and this was a documented bridge loan. That made some sense. Once again, our confirmation bias helped rationalize our concerns. Neither of us really understood these maneuvers, and we desperately wanted to believe the company would eventually go public as promised. We had a lot riding on it, after all.

This was the first of numerous requests from Lawrence or Conrad for money transfers over the next six months. Each request had what sounded like a legitimate reason behind it; there never seemed to be any cause for alarm. Legally, George could have refused to loan HMC any money, but, doing so would have meant defying Lawrence, which no one wanted to do. We trusted that he knew what was best for the company. Lawrence continued calling me with these requests; I would pass them on to George, and he would ensure the payment. This became so routine that eventually, we didn't even think twice about it.

We figured that as long as Craig's team was making sure

everything was in order for the final audit, we had nothing to worry about.

We were also pleased with the fact that Cascade Pointe was a money machine. Over six months, fifty accredited investors invested more than *twelve million* dollars. With our newly acquired understanding of what an accredited investor is, we were very impressed that so many of them invested in the white knight. These were all very smart people. At least, they were smart enough to have amassed a level of wealth that would allow them to invest in Cascade Pointe; there were no "little guys" allowed in the white knight. These facts not only put George and me at ease, they reassured the investor community, who all seemed even more excited now that there was a white knight to fund the company to get across the finish line.

The IR department phones continued to ring off the hook. The excitement and energy from the investors calling IR fueled the IR team, which in turn fueled the rest of the investors.

Occasionally we would get a call for a refund request. Most were turned down, but on at least three occasions, Lawrence or Conrad would authorize the refund. Lawrence wanted to silence the loudest complainers. He "didn't want any negative publicity just as we are approaching the finish line," as he would say.

It worked. Once the investor received their money back, they were never heard from again. They were the lucky ones.

PLANNING FOR OUR WEALTH

Many of us were dreaming of the day we would be able to sell our stock. Lawrence was generous about rewarding hard work with bonuses, which usually came in the form of stock. We preferred stock, actually, since we planned to sell it after opening day and enjoy the return. Each person on the IR team had growing portfolios, myself included.

Jackson had a pretty large database of former clients and friends, and he was selling a lot of HMC stock to them. One morning he and I were discussing our forthcoming wealth, and he asked if I had done anything to protect my assets. That concept was pretty foreign to me. Even when I sold my tech company during the dot com era, I didn't hire a financial planner or consider the idea of protecting our wealth.

Jackson encouraged me to find a local financial planner to help me create wealth strategies, so that the sudden influx of money would be protected from "financial predators in this litigious society," a phrase I started hearing often. On top of that, he assured me a good financial planner could also help minimize the tax liability.

It all made sense. I set out to find a financial planning firm, and ended up stumbling upon it out of nowhere. As we were all walking to a nice restaurant the next day for lunch, we walked right by a large sign at the entrance of a high-rise that said, "Wealth Strategies." I told the guys to go ahead to the restaurant and save me a seat.

The Wealth Strategies office suite was immediately on the left as I walked into the marble-floored lobby of the financial building. On the right was a Key Bank branch. It seemed obvious that Wealth Strategies was a very successful business that probably catered to the rich and famous in Bellevue. At least, that was the impression they created.

A professional receptionist greeted me. When I explained what I needed, she said I should speak directly with the owner, Edward, and scheduled an appointment for me for later in the week.

I left and joined the others for lunch. I had no idea at the time that the Illusion of Wealth Blind Spot was ingrained deeply into my worldview.

ILLUSION OF WEALTH BLIND SPOT

The American Dream is defined differently for each person, but most would agree that having financial peace of mind and enjoying 'the good life,' however that is defined, are important components.

What you don't realize is how the Illusion of Wealth Blind Spot influences good people to make bad choices.

First, you need to define wealth. For the purposes of understanding this blind spot, I'll just define 'wealth' as having more than enough money to live out your idea of the American Dream. Wealth does not have to mean being a millionaire or billionaire.

For a young family with current household earnings of $50,000 per year, wealth might simply mean reaching levels of $70,000 to $80,000 per year. That increase might allow them to afford the newer car, the larger house, the regular vacations, and a savings plan to put the kids through college.

For the young person in college eating Top Ramen, wealth might look like that $50,000 per year corporate job.

For others, wealth might in fact be defined as never having to work a day in their life.

However large the spread between where you are now and where you want to be financially, the blind spot grows in this illusion; it's in the subtly of your desire.

You think, "If I can reach this goal (you plug in your magic number here), we would be financially solvent, and enjoy the lifestyle we desire. We will have the financial peace of mind we crave."

This line of thinking is not based in reality. How can it be? You have not yet reached that place, so how can you know that when you get there you'll be truly at peace? You can't. In fact, many of those who *do* reach those illusory milestones find themselves facing a whole new set of problems.

The mere idea of reaching this arbitrary financial goal shapes your worldview, which in turn influences your decisions and behaviors.

The Illusion of Wealth blind spot can influence your decision to overlook potential dangers in accepting an employment opportunity. It can influence you to take greater investment risks than you should. It can influence individuals to embezzle or steal if the opportunity presents itself. Or, worst of all, it can influence you to sacrifice relationships with those you love.

Blind Spot Challenge: How high a value are you putting on money when making your major decisions?

BETTER-THAN-AVERAGE BLIND SPOT

When you read or hear statements like the above, your first inclination is to shrug it off. Your unconscious bias causes you to think you are better than the average person. But remember, everyone thinks that – and not everyone can be right. "There are a ton more studies[3] which demonstrate this tendency to rate oneself as above average: **ninety percent** of drivers think they are better than the average driver[4], and most students think they are more intelligent than the average student[5]."[29]

You think, "Other people might be tempted to embezzle or steal, but certainly not me!"

THE CORRUPTION EXPERIMENT

However, according to the results of a corruption experiment by behavioral scientist Daniel Ariely, 90% of the participants would steal or cheat given the right circumstances.

The experiment begins by inviting participants to roll a six-sided die. They are told that they can keep in dollars whatever number shows up on the roll of the die, either the top or the bottom side. They have to mentally pick the top or bottom before they roll, but they don't have to tell the researcher which side they chose until after the die is rolled. In other words, if the die is rolled and shows a two on the top, then the bottom would be a five. The participant then tells the researcher whether they chose the top (two) or the bottom (five). What do you think most people did? If they rolled a two and picked top, would they tell the researcher "top" and get only two dollars? Or, do they change their mind and say "bottom" to get five dollars? According to Ariely, after 20 rolls he finds that "people are incredibly lucky."[30]

He went on to further measure dishonesty by adding two versions of the experiment. In the first version, people were told there were two experiments: one of which would allow the participant to earn a maximum of four dollars, the other a maximum of forty dollars. The participant flipped a coin. No matter which side of the coin landed face up, the researcher

---

[29] Whittlestone, Jess (Nov 27, 2012) *Do you think you're better than average?* Retrieved from https://80000hours.org/2012/11/do-you-think-you-re-better-than-average/

[30] Retrieved from https://www.youtube.com/watch?v=2KyavuKmdNE

told the participant that, unfortunately, they would have a maximum of four dollars.

Then the researcher looks around and says, "Listen, my boss is not here today. So, I'll tell you what. You got three dollars to show up to the experiment. If you will give me these three dollars, I'll pretend you got the other coin flip." In essence, the researcher is asking for a bribe.

Ninety percent of the participants bribed the researcher in order to walk away with forty dollars instead of four.

The participants also starting cheating more. And, they started stealing.

As the participants rolled the die and told the researcher their choices, the researcher kept a tally of the results. After they finished all their rolls, the total points were summed up. If the total was twenty-three dollars, for example, the researcher handed the participant an envelope with fifty dollars in it. They told the participant to take out the amount of money they deserved and leave the balance in the envelope. Then they were to drop the envelope in a big box of other envelopes on the way out the door.

People would write twenty-three dollars on the envelope but take out more money than they deserved before dropping it in to the box.

Ariely explains in his video about the experiment, "If the person running the system is telling us that dishonesty is allowed, our understanding of what is acceptable changes instantly."

You find yourself in situations where you rationalize your actions as insignificant in the grand scheme of things. For instance, if your boss stocks up on office supplies from the supply cabinet at work, and then brings items home for personal use, you are much more likely to do the same. If you consciously think about this act, which most of the time you don't, you rationalize that everything is okay; after all, the boss is doing it, right?

I was speaking recently to a young man who just earned his Master's degree in a high-demand field of environmental studies. Though he is extremely bright, and would probably make a great employee, he has been largely unsuccessful securing work in his desired geographic location.

He commented, "I'm a bit discouraged. I spoke to several people who already work in this field. They told me I need to exaggerate my work experience on my job applications; otherwise, I won't even be considered. They were basically telling me to lie to the potential employer," he said, exasperated. "They said it's 'just how you have to roll if you want to get a government job.'"

He wrapped up by saying, "I refuse to be deceptive. But it is hard and discouraging. Maybe I just need to 'play the game!'"

Kudos to this young man for not compromising his own integrity, even though doing so might get him employed much faster. But how long will he withstand the pressure?

Good people can make bad choices when we succumb to ethical fading.

ETHICAL FADING

"Ethical fading is the tendency for otherwise ethical people to make unethical decisions, because the ethical implications have faded. For example, aspects of everyday work life – including goals, rewards, compliance systems, and informal pressures –

can contribute to ethical fading. These common features of organizations can blind us to the ethical implications of a decision, leading us, for example, to classify a decision as a 'business decision' rather than an 'ethical decision.'"[31]

In other words, you reclassify what should be ethical decisions by referring to them as something else altogether. You might use terms like "Just playing the game," "When in Rome," or "It's just the way we do it around here."

In the case of the young man, the longer he's out of work, and the more he hears industry professionals tell him to fabricate his application, the greater the chance of ethical fading. If he's not careful, he might just succumb to following suit because "that's just the way it's done."

"The organizational practices that contribute to ethical fading may be as subtle as differences in the language used to describe the decision. A case in point is Albert Speer, one of Adolf Hitler's government ministers and most trusted advisers. After the war, Speer admitted that by labeling himself as an "administrator" of Hitler's plan, he convinced himself that issues relating to human beings were not part of his job. This labeling allowed Speer to reclassify ethical decisions as business decisions, such that the ethical dimensions faded from the decision."[32]

Similarly, executives might not recognize ethical dilemmas when making important decisions that affect employees or customers, because they've categorized these business decisions as "protecting the stakeholders."

Employees might not realize they are making unethical de-

---

[31] Bazerman, Max H., Tenbrunsel, Ann E., *Blind Spots: Why we fail to do what's right and what to do about it.* Princeton University Press 2011, page acknowledgements, pg. 30
[32] Ibid, pg. 31

cisions when they think in terms of, "It's not my responsibility," or, "I didn't make up the policies."

Salespeople might be tempted to sell a customer more than they really need or want. Or, as in the case of the 2016 Wells Fargo scandal, they might even sell customers something they don't even know they are receiving. When your boss is pressuring you to meet a quota, it's easy to forget the ethical ramifications.

Ethical fading removes the concept that a decision is an ethical one. You become unaware that you are in the midst of an ethical dilemma.

When good people make bad choices, it's not always because they were aware of the moral issue at hand and chose to make a bad choice. Sometimes good people are simply unaware that the choices they are making are, in fact, unethical.

CREATING WEALTH STRATEGIES

I finally met with Edward at Wealth Strategies on Friday morning in his marble-floored office. He was a clean-cut, small-framed man, in his early thirties; he dressed professionally and was extremely warm and personable, very easy to talk to. He seemed like an overall down-to-earth good guy who was smart with financial affairs. After introductions and small talk, we got down to business.

"So, tell me about your current financial situation, and how I can help."

I explained my role in the company, and how my stock portfolio would be worth in excess of $2 million in just a couple of months.

"So, Edward, the last time I had a stock portfolio, I managed it on my own and ended up losing almost everything," I explained. "I don't want that to happen again!"

"Well, what you're describing is very unique for me," Edward replied tentatively. "You have stock in a private company now that is getting ready to become a public company; I'm not sure how to handle that. Let me contact my broker dealer representative and get some advice."

I was encouraged. He seemed like he sincerely wanted to help, and I knew I needed the support. "Oh, by the way," he added as we were wrapping up, "can other people still buy stock in this company?"

"I believe so," I said, curious. "Are you thinking of offering this to your clients?"

"No, but I'm thinking I might like to invest in the company myself. Is there anyone else there I might speak with about it?"

"Let me see what I can do," I said, and that was the end of that meeting.

But it wasn't long until he called.

"Kevin, I would like to invest $5,000 in the company," he said over the phone on Monday. I could tell he was trying to restrain the excitement in his voice. "I don't need to speak to anyone else. I've read enough online to satisfy my concerns. What's the next step?"

An hour later he came to our office and wrote the check. He also told me that he'd received approval to "take me on" as a new client prior to the public offering. I was elated!

As I reflect back on that day, my head was completely in

the clouds. Edward accepting me as a client just reinforced my delusion that becoming a multimillionaire was imminent.

I was so smitten by the Illusion of Wealth Blind Spot that it could have rightly been called the *delusion* of wealth. I was feeling incredibly proud – or maybe arrogant is a better word – about having a personal wealth manager who would help me invest my portfolio and increase my wealth even more. On top of that, I also learned that I needed "asset protection vehicles" to protect my new wealth from "predatory litigation."

Those are the phrases I learned from Jackson. He and I were discussing our portfolios and the imminent IPO, and he suggested that I open an offshore account. He explained that offshore accounts are legal, which is true, as long as income taxes are paid appropriately. They are, however, usually reserved for the wealthy. Fortunate for me, he knew Frank Yantze, the owner of an Oregon-based company that sets up offshore accounts for qualified, wealthy individuals. More importantly, Frank was in partnership with Terry Neal, the foremost expert on offshore corporations, and author of *The Offshore Solution*. Jackson had read his book and was impressed.

THE OFFSHORE CORPORATION

When Jackson made the call to Frank and introduced me, we spoke for about 20 minutes. He introduced me to the concept of IBC's, Offshore International Business Corporations. That sounded impressive; setting up an IBC would provide nearly impenetrable asset protection.

He explained that they would first set up a Nevada corporation for the client. Then they would set up two Nevis/Saint Kitts IBC's. Nevis/St Kitts are Caribbean islands, known for being an offshore tax haven. The client would then wire transfer funds to the Nevada corporation, which in turn wires it to the first IBC. Once the funds were in Nevis/Saint Kitts, that

The Availability Blind Spot influences you to accept more readily available information, and to ignore the more difficult-to-find information. There is so much information available these days that we often suffer from information overload; the easier information is to access, the more it affects your decisions.

In my case, I had Terry Neal's book, plus Jackson and Frank's opinions in the matter. That was much easier to digest than sifting through the myriad of articles and blogs, trying to verify which ones were credible and which ones weren't.

Access to information has never been easier, but it's also much more difficult to decipher which information is accurate and valid – not hype and hyperbole. The 'fake news' phenomenon is a perfect example of this. Which means it's also more important than ever to be skeptical, but not cynical, of the information you see, read, and hear.

The problem is, information that is easier to obtain is not necessarily the most accurate. The more reliable information might be more obscure; or a subscription or purchase might be required. For some scientific studies, you can only acquire their original documents by purchasing them. Or the accurate information is so complicated that it really does require an expert to understand it.

That was the case with the offshore IBCs. Terry Neal explained it in lay terms, and it made sense, but of course the smarter move might have been to consult an attorney who specialized in asset protection. Ah, the benefits of hindsight!

FIND THE SOURCE

We all have opinions and convictions about what we believe to be true; I'm not suggesting that you throw the baby out with the bathwater. But you *should* challenge yourself to be more skeptical about the information you accept as true. Whether the information supports your bias or contradicts it, being skeptical is a healthier approach to formulating better beliefs and decisions.

Ironically, in the IR department, one of our main tasks was to verify the investments. Lawrence used to tell us that he wanted us to see the source documents. When doing research, you can mitigate the Availability Blind Spot by *looking for the source*. Who is reporting the information? What are their sources? Look for the citations in the article. Follow the links or to find the original source. Is that source widely accepted as credible? Who did the survey? Who conducted the clinical study? Did that person or group have anything to gain from a positive outcome? Could there be a bias in the study that would cause the results to be suspect?

These are hard questions. They take time to resolve. Time, you usually don't have. Hence, you use the easy route to obtain information to make your decisions and formulate your opinions.

I understand the lack of time and the sense of overwhelm in researching real facts. But, at the very least, we should all agree to back down on voicing strong convictions, and agree instead to take a more flexible stance.

What if we all made a habit of saying, "Based on what I think I know, this is what I currently believe. However, I'm open to new perspectives"? There would probably be a lot more quality communication, and a lot fewer mistakes.

Action Tip: Maintain this attitude… "Based on what I think I know, this is what I currently believe. However, I am open to new perspectives."

PERSPECTIVES

I'm a professional member of the National Speakers Association, and served in the role of President of the Oregon Chapter. One thing I've discovered is that professional speakers are hired largely because of three things: their unique perspectives, fascinating stories, and presentation skills.

All of us have a unique perspective. That's what makes the world, and people in it, so fascinating. But it's important to realize that your unique perspective is just that: "your" perspective. It may align with the masses, or it may be quite contrary to the norm. Wherever your perspective lies on the continuum, you would do well to be open to the idea that *you might very well be wrong*.

You know that your worldview filters how you perceive the world around you. What you don't often think about is how you are affected by subtle and often undetectable influences, pressures and biases that affect your decisions and influence the perspectives and beliefs to which you hold dear.

Be open to new perspectives. It will help you in the long run, more than you know.

THE OFFSHORE CONSULTANT

After reading Terry Neal's book, I contacted Frank Yantze and purchased my own IBC, then arranged for some of my company stock to be transferred there. The plan was to eventually liquidate my portfolio, so the funds would be held and protected offshore. After filing the appropriate tax returns, I would repatriate some of it back to the USA while leaving other funds offshore and investing them in international markets.

With Edward, all set to help with wealth strategies, and the new IBC's in place, I was feeling much smarter than I actually was. The illusion of wealth was feeding my overinflated ego; I was not in a healthy place. And, to be honest, it only got worse. The wealthier I thought I was becoming, the more I lost touch with reality. I was living under the delusion of being a multimillionaire, even though the stock hadn't yet become validated through the IPO.

One of the rules of owning an IBC is to keep it a secret. But, as you might guess, I was so proud of my new investment protection prowess that I could hardly stand not talking about it.

One day, not long after I'd finished setting up the IBC's, a substantial investor named Tom called IR for an update.

"Hi, Tom, nothing new to report," I said before he could utter a word. I knew why he was calling. He called weekly, eager to hear the words we were all waiting to hear: *The IPO is happening now!*"

He laughed at my introduction, but still wanted to make conversation. "So, what else is going on with you?"

"I've been busy getting my portfolio under management," I said enthusiastically. "I want to be ready for the tax consequences and investment opportunities that will ensue."

"Yeah, I've been wondering about stuff like that," he said. "Any tips?"

"Well, as a matter of fact, yes…" How could I resist? This was my chance to impress Tom, whom I understood to be a sophisticated, accredited investor, as defined by the SEC code.

I explained to Tom what I'd learned from Frank Yantze and Terry Neal's book, and he was thrilled. He wrote down the names and said he was going to reach out to Frank right away, and even order the book! It felt great that I could steer a fellow investor in the right direction.

This wasn't the only time. In fact, it started happening more and more. I would find ways to bring up the subject with some of the more astute investors, and they were all appropriately impressed, and appreciative. Many of them started working with Frank for their own asset protection vehicles.

After about the fifth referral I sent to Frank, it dawned on me to ask him for a referral fee. If I was going to send so many people his way, why not pick up a little extra pocket money for the trouble?

THE FINDER'S FEE

"Hi Frank, this is Kevin McCarthy," I said after his secretary transferred the call to him.

"Hi Kevin, what can I do for you?"

"Well, I had this crazy thought… Since I've been sending you clients, and will likely send quite a few more, how would you feel about paying me a finder's fee?" It was a bold ask, but what did I have to lose?

"Funny you should ask," he said, "I was just thinking the same thing. But I'm thinking we should set you up as one of our sales reps and split the fee with you. We usually offer this to attorneys and CPA's, but as the head of the IR department, it makes sense for you to learn all you can about the products. This way you can help your clients and get rewarded for doing so. How does that sound?" Frank's response was calculated – he was prepared for the offer.

"That sounds really good!" I said happily. "What are the next steps?"

Frank said he would have his sales trainer, Bret, give me a call. Once I was trained, I would be able to handle all of the paperwork for the investors that were interested in IBC's.

Bret was based in Utah. He contacted me to schedule four telephone training sessions, and I decided to record each of them so I could use them as a reference.

What I learned about the offshore business and investing world was mind-boggling. On one hand, it felt like secrets reserved for the rich and famous. There were tax and asset shelter maneuvers that were complicated and expensive. But, if you wanted to make it nearly impossible for someone to discover all of your assets, these maneuvers were a good way of doing it. On the other hand, I also learned that there is a fine line between tax avoidance and tax evasion. The former is legal when done right. The latter is very much illegal. After these lessons, it was easy to see how someone could quickly cross that legal line, intentionally or unintentionally.

Later in the case, the FBI ended up with my recordings. One of the agents even commented, "That training was an excellent lesson on how to evade taxes."

I don't know if his comments were completely true, or just a biased perspective. In fact, I don't know if anything in Terry Neal's book was accurate. Maybe the entire IBC process as Terry Neal described it was illegal. Maybe Frank, Terry and their team were just perpetrating their own scam to sell illegal IBC's.

Incidentally, Frank and Terry both showed up at the prison, Federal Correctional Institution, Sheridan, during the last year of my sentence. Apparently, they'd been under investigation during the same timeframe that Lawrence was being investigated. Unbeknownst to any of us, the government had a simultaneous, separate investigation and an open case against them.

I believe the main difference between legally or illegally enjoying all the benefits of offshore corporations, investing, and bank accounts, is whether or not you are reporting all of your income to the IRS. Unfortunately, the process is very complex and risky; knowing when you've crossed the line is difficult to discern. According to *Investopedia*, "Offshore investing is often demonized in the media, which paints a picture of investors stashing their money with some illegal company located on an obscure Caribbean island where the tax rate is next to nothing. While it's true that there will always be instances of shady offshore deals, the vast majority of offshore investing is perfectly legal.[34]"

I do know this: if I am ever fortunate enough to be in a position to want to protect my assets again, I will hire an attorney to handle the process. Then again, now that I think about it… I met a lot of attorneys in prison.

SUMMER OF DREAMS

The summer of 2001 was exciting. The Seattle weather was beautiful. Investors were flocking to be part of Cascade Pointe. The IPO was imminent and now scheduled for the Fall – again. Our portfolios had grown substantially. Most of the IR team would end up with more than one million dollars after the IPO opened at the expected $18-$22 per share. Enthusiasm and loyalty were high.

A small group decided to visit an RV show in downtown Seattle. It was fun to dream as you walked through motor homes selling for $500,000 and more. Most of us were not interested, but a couple people who had healthy portfolios set their sights on buying one of these fancy coaches once they sold their stock. These were the same people who were going

---

[34] Investopedia staff. Retrieved from
http://www.investopedia.com/articles/02/020602.asp?lgl=myfinance-layout-no-ads

to, "use their newfound wealth for everyone, and not let the money change their own lifestyle." Funny how quickly we forget.

I wasn't any different. Motor homes were not my thing, but our next outing was the boat show. Now we're talkin'!

I was dreaming of the yachts that ranged from $350,000 on up. By the end of the show I had one picked out: a floating, custom-built home on the inside. A real entertainment craft. And can you guess what came out of my mouth? "Wouldn't this be a great gift to traveling missionaries to invite them for an R&R cruise?"

Even while I was aware that other investors were justifying their greed with altruism, I succumbed to the very same thing.

It's easier to see the blind spots in others than to see them in yourself.

FINALLY! THE HOLY GRAIL

Summer was coming to a close when I received the most exciting call I'd ever received from Lawrence.

"Kevin, I need you, George and Dave to make a trip to the Island tonight to pick up the final paperwork. This is it, Kevin! We're about to cross the finish line. The final paperwork will be ready late this afternoon. This is your chance to finally see the holy grail. I need George to sign it as Managing Partner for Cascade Pointe, LLC, but the paperwork is still top secret, so, just the three of you. You will have one hour to review and sign the document. Meet Jessica at the Chevron station near the office. She will hand you the non-descript envelope. Find a place to park. Read it. Bring it back to her an hour later. Can you do that?" Everything was very cloak-and-dagger.

"Wow! Absolutely! This is awesome!" I said, about to burst out of my skin with excitement. "Thank you so much for making this finally happen. We won't tell a soul until the stock is public."

"No!" he said with zeal. "I want you to share the news and let *everyone* know you've seen the paperwork, and that we are about to launch. I want you to throw the biggest party tomorrow; contact our closest friends and investors. Rent a huge yacht loaded with party food and beverages! Get everyone together tomorrow, and spend the day celebrating. Monday is going to be a big day for all of us!"

I called George and shared the news. He immediately conferenced Dave (a mutual friend) into the call. Craig's accountant was too busy to manage the books effectively, and George wanted someone local that he knew and trusted to ensure everything was "on the up and up," as he put it. So, just like that, George hired Dave as CFO for Cascade Point.

THE FERRY RIDE

The call came in around ten o'clock on Friday morning. The party was supposed to happen the next day, so George had the Cascade Pointe administrator make all the arrangements. She rented a yacht, made all the party arrangements and personally invited the top investors.

The IR team, the Cascade team, and all the investors who heard the news were flying high with emotion. We were finally at that infamous *finish line*! The long days, the emotional roller coaster, and the cease and desist were all behind us. We were about to be celebrating the victory of taking the company public. I wondered if all IPO's went through this much drama behind the scenes.

The last step for us was to get on the 4:30 ferry to

Bainbridge Island so we could review the IPO documents for the first, and last, time.

"Unbelievable!" That was the only word George and I could say, simultaneously, on the call.

The three of us jumped in our car and boarded the Washington state ferry from Seattle to Bainbridge Island. It was a 30-minute ride, exciting to say the least. We were giddy with anticipation.

The ferry landed. We followed the directions to the Chevron station and saw a black Cadillac Escalade parked conspicuously along the side of the building. As we approached, a beautiful woman exited the vehicle with an envelope. It was Jessica. She worked for Lawrence. We weren't exactly sure what she did or what her title was, but it didn't matter, did it? This was happening!

I didn't even have to get out of the car. Like a scene from a spy movie, she slipped the envelope through the window and said she would meet us back here in one hour.

We grabbed the envelope and drove off. From the back seat, Dave opened the envelope and pulled out a stack of papers. "Gentlemen, it's going to take more than an hour to read through everything," he said as he looked it over. "George, I suppose we can just review the highlights, then have you sign. But I'd kind of like to read the entire document thoroughly. Why don't we find a copier and make our own copy?"

We all thought it was a great idea. We agreed the copy would stay with us and no one would know we had it, especially not Lawrence; we knew he wouldn't want them copied for fear they would be leaked to the investor community. Lawrence didn't trust anyone, not even us. That was part of his manipulative and controlling nature.

So, we figured we would simply destroy the copy after we'd had a chance to read it. It was a plan.

So, we drove to the local library, expecting to find a copier. However, it was now after 5:00 pm and the library was closed. We tried a couple of real estate offices, but they were closed, too. Our last effort paid off: we remembered that some Safeway stores had coin-operated copiers. We lucked out, because the only Safeway on the island was nearby, and it had a copier.

We nervously entered the store. The island was small, and we didn't want to bump into Lawrence or anyone who might recognize us. We made our way to the back of the store and copied all 124 pages.

Once we were done, we drove the original back to the Chevron and met Jessica. We handed her the envelope and left, heading to a place around the corner to park and start reading our copy. Within minutes, the mood in the car went from exuberance to disillusionment. Our hearts sank. We felt as if someone had stuck a dagger through our hopes and dreams.

The paperwork was not the IPO paperwork. It was merely a merger and acquisition document between Cascade Pointe and HMC. It had nothing to do with the IPO. In fact, it was so poorly written, we questioned its legitimacy.

The ferry ride and drive home seemed to take forever. We were speechless. Whenever any of us spoke, it was mostly negative. We wondered if the IPO would ever happen. Was it possible that the IPO was not real? Could this all be a scam? We had thought we'd be able to see the announcement on national news on Monday, and be able to watch the stock soar on opening day. Obviously, *that* was not going to happen.

I called Lawrence, and when he didn't answer, left a discouraged voice message. George called his assistant and had her cancel the yacht and the party. None of it made any sense.

Lawrence called us back just as we arrived in Bellevue where George and Dave had parked their cars.

"Why are you guys so discouraged?" he cried over the phone. "That's crazy! This should be cause for celebration. I didn't tell you anything about IPO paperwork. This is the merger document that is needed for the IPO to happen. This is the final piece of the puzzle! What you just signed is critical to completing the process. There is no reason to be discouraged. I'm disappointed you canceled the party, but hang in there – don't give up on me now! We've fought hard to get here and we're almost done. Are you still with me? I need to know if you are still with me – Kevin?" Lawrence spoke with such vision and conviction it was hard to remain discouraged.

I mustered up an answer, "We're still with you Lawrence. We just thought this was something that it wasn't. So, when *will* the IPO happen? What do we tell everyone?"

"You know I can't give you a real date. I'm not allowed. Only the lawyers, accountants and brokers have that information. But we're very close. This was the last document that we needed to complete the package. Stay focused and we'll all win very soon! Okay?"

"Okay," I said, trying hard to sound enthusiastic.

George, Dave and I parted ways for the evening and agreed to regroup on Monday. We were wobbly with discouragement and didn't have much more to say.

On Monday, we all went to lunch to debrief from the Holy Grail trip.

We all agreed that even though we were discouraged, we

needed to "keep the faith." That was one of many of Lawrence's favorite sayings, and we adopted it. We reconciled that we didn't see the big picture like Lawrence did. He obviously could see all the puzzle pieces coming together from his vantage point, and we couldn't. We were desperate to find something good to hang on to. George said, "We can cope if we have hope." And so that's what we created for ourselves — hope. Lawrence was masterful at keeping us focused on the finished line, but we were pretty good at doing it ourselves as well. At least a few of us were.

CHAPTER FIVE:
CRASH AND BURN

OUT OF MONEY

Three weeks after the holy grail letdown, Conrad visited IR. He walked into my office and closed the door.

"Hey, Kevin, there's no easy way to tell you this, but... the company is out of money. No one is getting paid today." His voice almost cracked with despair.

"What do you mean 'out of money?'" I exclaimed.

"Jackson's investor backed out," he explained. "We have no cash on hand right now. We need more investments if we are going to move forward. We need everyone calling their friends and families right away, asking them to invest more. It's critical."

"That's ridiculous! You want me to tell my team they're not getting paid, then ask them to call their friends and family for money? That's not going to happen." I was practically steaming with indignation.

"You can just deal with Lawrence about that, then," he said, and with that, walked out the door.

I couldn't believe my ears. No paycheck? No money in the company? I just sat in my chair dazed. My brain was in a fog. "I need to call George," I finally thought to myself. But before I could dial his number, my phone rang. It was Lawrence.

"Kevin, I need you to calm down. This is just a setback. We've been through many setbacks together, haven't we?"

"I suppose we have. But running out of *money*?"

"Listen, Jackson has another investor who's checking us out and considering providing the final 3.7 million that we need to cross the finish line. That's it," he added, using every bit of his power of persuasion. "One last investment and we're done. Don't give up on me now, Kevin – I need you focused."

"When is this investment coming in?" I demanded. "How long do you expect us to work without a paycheck?"

"Soon. Let everyone know they will get paid the minute we get the money. Are you with me, Kevin?"

"Yeah, I suppose we've come too far to throw in the towel now. I'll let the team know. But Lawrence – I have no idea how they will take the news."

"Keep me posted," was all he said, then he hung up without a goodbye.

I think I was still in shock. Lawrence's call calmed me down a bit, but it still felt like someone had punched me in the gut and knocked the wind out of me. It was despair.

I called George immediately.

"Hey good buddy, what's new?" George answered with his normal, glad-to-hear-your-voice.

"George, this is not a good call, my friend," I said soberly.

George hesitated. "Tell me."

"Conrad is probably on his way to your office to break the news. Apparently, the company is out of money, and no one is getting paid today."

"What?! Oh, dear God. This is not good. Kev… this is not a good day."

"I know. I don't know what to think. I feel like I've lost hope again. I haven't even told the others yet. What should we do?" I was desperate for George to cheer me up and bring us back to a place of hope.

But all he said was, "Kev, I gotta go. Call ya later." And he hung up.

He needed time to process the news. I needed more time, too, but I didn't have that luxury. Stuart opened my door and asked if Conrad had dropped off the paychecks.

I motioned to him to go back in the other room as I followed him out my door. Then I broke the news to everyone.

Now everyone was depressed. My answer to the barrage of questions was the same: "I have no idea." I didn't know if I was going to quit. I didn't know if the company would survive the drought. I didn't know if we would ever see what could in essence be our final paychecks. I had no answers.

No one was in the mood to do any work. So, we shut off the phones. I sent everyone home.

Over the course of the next few days, most of the staff called to say they quit. I couldn't blame them; they were living paycheck-to-paycheck and needed to find another job. George and Dave of Cascade Pointe, as well as Jackson, Stuart and myself from the IR department, all decided to stick it out as long as we could.

Another payday came and went with no paychecks and no investments. Everyone was focused on Jackson and his investor.

I think the main reason we stuck around was because Jackson assured us his investment firm was the real deal. As a former stockbroker, he was very connected to the investment community. He explained that this investment group was very serious about investing the final 3.7 million; it was just taking time. That was the thread of hope we needed to hang in there a little longer. But not all of us did.

After missing a couple more paychecks, Stuart quit. Dave soon followed suit, though as a dear friend of George's, he said he would make himself available if anyone had questions. George and I never saw Jackson again. At the time, we assumed he was working on securing the needed investment. We had no idea we were about to be absolutely blindsided.

By October 2001, the IR department no longer existed. I was fielding select investor calls from the few who had my mobile number. There wasn't much to report. I rarely spoke with Lawrence; he was probably getting tired of my demands to see the IPO paperwork.

When I called him, it would almost always go to voicemail. Most of my messages were not returned. When he did call back, it was to tell me that the deal with Jackson's investors was "getting close." He was hoping to inspire hope, but at this point it wasn't working. My faith in Lawrence was fading quickly. With every excuse, I lost more and more hope.

I didn't have much going on at this point. Other than the phone calls from investors, and conversations with George, I was pretty bored. Earlier in the year I had met a couple of inner-city Christian ministers, Simon and Raymond, and one positive aspect of this period was that I got to spend some quality time with them. Simon was a pastor of a small church, and Raymond was one of his non-staff leaders. Both had dreams of leading big revivals.

We met when they came to our home to pick up a large roll of carpet we were donating, and we really hit it off. Since I had time on my hands, I would drive to Simon's home or we would meet at a coffee shop several times a week. We were dreaming and making plans to develop an old-style tent revival outreach ministry. If and when the IPO finally happened, I would gladly fund this start-up ministry, and even help Simon's church with a significant financial donation. Materialism Blind Spot still fully engaged.

This ministry was a nice distraction. But, once the calendar rolled into November, I was ready to quit working for Lawrence and give up all hope for an IPO. I was going to cut my losses and give everything up. Yet, like so many times before, just when we needed it the most, Lawrence called with good news.

"Kevin, get ready. We're done! Jackson's investors are moving forward. It will take 30 days or so to work out all the details, but once we get the paperwork signed and their funds deposited, I will make sure everyone gets paid what they're owed, including the auditors and legal team. My attorneys assured me that once everyone is paid – them first, of course – we will pull the trigger. It will be a day of massive celebration! Let everyone know, okay? Okay, Kevin? Are you still with me?"

Lawrence spoke with a level of energy and enthusiasm I hadn't heard for a while. Something was energizing him, but I wasn't sure I bought it.

I acknowledged him, and he hung up the phone.

I immediately called George and shared the news. We were both skeptical. But if anyone could put together a large investment deal, it would be Jackson, and we knew it. This gave us another boost of hope. Just enough to last a couple weeks, until the next call from Lawrence.

THE SMOKING GUN

Lawrence called with more instructions to relay to George.

"Kevin, George is going to receive a fax from the Washington Department of Financial Institutions. He needs to sign it and fax it back to them so we can finish the process. Okay?" This time, Lawrence spoke in a strange tone, a tone he had never used with me before: he sounded nervous.

"Uh, sure," I said. "I'll let him know. What's the fax all about?" I was curious — what on earth could make Lawrence talk like this?

"Remember when I asked you to set up the white knight? Well, in order to satisfy the state's investigation, they want proof that I am not involved in Cascade Pointe," he explained. "They want George to sign an affidavit attesting to that fact."

"But, Lawrence, it's really no secret that you completely run Cascade Pointe," I exclaimed. "He'll be lying if he signs that document. I don't think he'll do it, and I don't even want to ask him to!"

"Kevin, he needs to sign the document or we're done. We can't cross the finish line until the state is satisfied that our white knight is compliant and able to follow through on the rescission offering. He needs to sign the affidavit. Period. Let me know when it's signed."

Lawrence hung up. No room for discussion.

I was in shock. I called George immediately and explained

what I had been told. He, too, went into shock. We were both speechless.

I did not ask him to sign the document. For the first time working with Lawrence, we had a clear moral dilemma. In our minds, everything had been 'business as usual' up 'til now. We didn't understand the big picture, and whenever there were setbacks Lawrence had a reasonably sound explanation. But this was different: he was asking George to swear under oath that Lawrence had no influence over Cascade Pointe.

If George signed the document, he knew he would be breaking the law. If he refused, he might be the single reason why five thousand investors would be at risk.

After trying to reason through what to do for about five minutes, George conferenced Dave into the call. He had the same reaction as us, and was speechless.

In hindsight it seems like a simple answer – don't sign the document, right? The problem is we suffer from the 20/20 Hindsight Blind Spot.

20/20 HINDSIGHT BLIND SPOT

The 20/20 Hindsight Blind Spot is when you look back at a decision you made and think to yourself that you knew the right decision all along, but simply made a poor choice. The truth is you probably didn't really know. If you had, you might have made that obvious choice. But you made a poor decision instead, thinking, in the context of the moment, that it really was the best decision.

SERIOUS MORAL DILEMMA

With regard to the affidavit, in the craziness of the moment, we had no idea what the right decision would be. Consider our line of reasoning: on the one hand, George signs the document falsifying the information in hopes that all the promises of going public would come to pass. It seemed like a question of the greater good. If he signs the document and satisfies the state and the company goes public, everyone comes out a winner – conscience notwithstanding.

But, of course, he'd run the risk that if he signed the document and the company didn't go public, then the State's investigation might uncover the truth about Lawrence's involvement, and cause legal ramifications for George – and probably Dave and me as well.

However, if he refused to sign the document, then the company not going public would be a sure thing – and everybody would lose.

He should not have signed the document. That's obvious now. But in that moment, after so much time and effort, after all of our dreams of wealth and the "little guy" investors we *knew* were counting on us, it didn't seem obvious at all. We concluded that we had about a ninety-percent confidence rate in Lawrence and the company. We believed that the IPO was legitimate, and would take place once the State officials were done with their investigation and the rescission offering had been completed.

We did not want to be responsible for killing the entire project. George signed the document, and faxed it back to the Washington Department of Financial Institutions, the state's version of the Federal SEC.

I called Lawrence and let him know. He was pleased.

We never heard another word about the document. We thought we had done the right thing; we thought we were moving closer to the IPO. Then, a few weeks later, George received an eighteen-page fax addressed to him and Cascade Pointe. He called me in a panic.

THE NIGERIAN SCAM

I answered George's call. It was December 18, 2001.

"Hey buddy, what's up?" I asked, always glad to hear from George.

"Kev, oh my God! I am beside myself. Freaked out. I just received an eighteen-page fax. I think Jackson is trying to scam Lawrence!"

"What do you mean?" I asked. This seemed way out of left field. "How could Jackson be trying to scam Lawrence?"

Jackson had been tasked by Lawrence to raise the "final" $2.4 million that was needed for operations, the audits, the legal team and the SEC filing. Once he raised that money, we were done – that's what he was told, anyway. That's when we'd cross the finish line.

We were all counting on Jackson, with his connections, to be able to pull off this fundraising, but before this fax we hadn't heard from him for weeks.

It was addressed to George, but the cover letter was addressed to Jackson. It was a fax confirming a $3.7 million commitment to invest funds in Cascade Pointe. But, before the investor would wire the funds, they required a $250,000 deposit to be wired to them to cover the costs of all the wire transfers. That request sounded fishy, and smelled like a scam all by itself. But the real scam was that the investment commitment was from the Nigerian government. It was obvious, blatant deception.

If you haven't heard of the Nigerian government scam, you can simply visit the FBI's website and read all about it.

The documents looked very official. We immediately concluded that Jackson, whose name was referenced in the fax cover sheet, had fabricated this Nigerian scam to steal $250,000 from Lawrence and Cascade Pointe.

George and I called Lawrence immediately and explained the fax. His response threw us both into a tailspin.

"Don't worry about Jackson," he said. "Just do as the paperwork is asking. If Jackson is really stealing the money, he'll get his when the time comes. But, for now, we can't have anything upset the forward movement of the project. We are right here at the finish line. I don't need a scuttlebutt right before we finish."

Lawrence sounded as if he already knew about the fax, and proceeded to authorize the wire transfer of $250,000.

He was in on it!

That was it for George and me. We decided we were not carrying out any more of Lawrence's wishes unless we could see the real paperwork, the S-1 filing for the SEC public offering. It didn't work, though; Lawrence continued to refuse to let us see the "top secret" paperwork – the real Holy Grail.

THE FIRST FBI VISIT

Two days later, I happened to be home early in the afternoon, when two FBI agents rang the doorbell. They were polite, and asked if they could come inside and talk with me about Lawrence. I obliged. I expected them to introduce themselves as Agent Johnson and Agent Johnson. They didn't.

We sat in my living room. We had two full size couches facing each other with a coffee table in between. I was on one couch and the two agents were on the other.

They revealed there was an ongoing investigation into Lawrence and HMC for stock fraud. They wanted to know how long I had worked for him, and what my responsibilities were. So, I told them.

Then they asked more. "Maybe you can help clear up a mystery for us. Once the cease and desist was issued, we assumed the operations would shut down, and everyone would quit working with him. Why are you and all the others still there?"

"The IPO," I explained easily. "We are all waiting for the IPO, which he said is imminent. Thousands of us have invested hard-earned dollars in the company, and want to see it succeed. That's why we're all still here."

"Kevin, there is *no* IPO paperwork," one of the agents proclaimed. "There never has been, and never will be!"

I must have gone pale or something, because I later learned from the same agent that they could tell from the look on my face that I had no idea this was a scam. They even testified to the prosecutor on my behalf.

After they left, my heart sank more than I can say. I shared the information with George and he shared in my misery. When Rachel came home later that day, I filled her in on the details of the FBI conversation.

She didn't seem overly surprised. Though she was a bit shocked that they had come to our house, she had always had that gut instinct that this was too good to be true.

"Now what?" she asked.

"I don't know," I said, discouraged and skeptical. "I need to call Lawrence."

"You need to tell Lawrence to take a hike! I'm tired of him controlling you and being in our lives," she said fiercely. She'd always known.

"I know. I know. Me too!" I sighed.

I was dreading a call to Lawrence. *Dreading* it. What could I say? How would he respond? But I needed to see what he had to say about the FBI visit – and what they'd said about the IPO paperwork. It took me a day to muster the courage to call, but the next morning, I did.

"Lawrence, hey. This is Kevin," I said, trying to speak with as much positivity as I could. If we ever called Lawrence without being positive, we would get an earful of "keep the faith."

"Hey, two FBI agents came by my house yesterday, and said there is no IPO paperwork. Why would they say that if it wasn't true?" I demanded.

"Kevin, they have no idea what they are talking about. Of course they would tell you that. They're following orders from the Washington DFI, trying to shake everyone up! No one has seen the paperwork except for the attorneys, auditors and a few key people at the stock brokerage." He explained everything so smoothly, as if he'd expected my call.

"Well, I really need to see the paperwork myself," I said forcefully. "Are you going to make that happen?"

"Listen, right after the holidays, when we finally cross the finish line, everyone will see it. Hang in there! Nobody said this would be easy! Don't give up on me now!" He abruptly hung up.

I didn't really believe him, but at this point, there was nothing I could do but wait. Wait for the FBI investigation to continue, wait for this farcical finish line to find us, wait to see what would happen. It was a horrible, stress-filled Christmas. George and I lost all hope.

But it was to get worse.

THE KNOCK ON THE DOOR

I survived those holidays by finding solace with my loving family.

When times would get tough, our motto was, "We always have each other." We celebrated the Christmas season as best we could under the circumstances. We decorated the house, decorated a Christmas tree; shopped and wrapped presents for each other. The kids had no idea about the stresses Rachel and I were dealing with, and that's the way we wanted it. Why ruin Christmas?

We hosted a party for friends and family. We sang carols. On the surface, it was another joyous holiday together. We *tried* to not think about Lawrence and the company, but that was impossible. Both were always on my mind.

The new year rolled in. Then, on January 7, 2002, around seven o'clock in the morning, Rachel and I were just waking up when we heard a loud knock on the door. Our kids were getting ready for school, so our son, Chris, answered it.

He yelled upstairs, "Dad! There are a bunch of people in suits here to see you!"

I got dressed and opened the bedroom door. The same two FBI agents, plus another four people, were in the foyer.

I went downstairs and asked what was going on. They handed me a subpoena, and explained they were searching for anything and everything I had in my possession that related to Lawrence or the company. They especially wanted to know where I kept my secret recordings. Apparently, someone tipped them off that I had recordings of some of my telephone calls, which I did.

I had started recording conversations with Lawrence earlier in the year because he was so hard to understand. He spoke extremely fast and often used terminology that I didn't understand, but if I asked him to repeat or explain himself he became irritated and questioned my ability to do my job. So, rather than create problems, I simply recorded the calls and listened to them at a reduced speed. It helped.

But near the end, once we suspected Lawrence was in on the Jackson deal, I was even more careful, and recorded every call. Something felt wrong, and I wanted to document what he was asking me – and all of us – to do.

The FBI secured all the micro cassette tapes – more than twenty of them – and had them all transcribed. Later, as their star witness, it was my job to listen to the recordings while reading the transcripts in order to correct any errors. My attorney told me they had trouble understanding Lawrence as well. It was like he had his own language, and I had learned how to interpret him.

The offshore training tapes were included in the batch, which apparently amused the FBI agents.

PUBLIC DEFENDER

After the FBI left, I contacted a criminal defense attorney. At that moment, I had no idea if I was in trouble, but I didn't want to take any chances. I paid the attorney a retainer, and he agreed to look into the case and let me know if I was a suspect.

As it turned out, I was a target of the investigation. He explained that meant I was not yet a suspect, but they were looking into my involvement. The attorney explained that he would not be able to represent me, because I could not afford it.

Out of the kindness of his heart, he made some calls and was able to get me assigned to a federal public defender right away. Usually an indictment or arrest would be needed to be assigned a public defender, but he had a friend in their office who pulled some strings.

"Great!" I said to myself. "A public defender. I'm in trouble now."

Public defenders are generally not regarded in the best light compared to a private practice attorney. I wasn't excited about being assigned to Carol, but in the end, she turned out to be a great attorney. My assumptions were all wrong.

MEETING WITH CAROL

I had numerous meetings with the public defender, Carol, over the next several weeks. She needed all the facts of the case. What's more, she needed to know if I could be trusted – and whether I was guilty or innocent.

The first time we met, Carol seemed cordial enough. I initially assumed that, as a public defender, she would be more of a paper-pusher, not really concerned with my future. And she did admit that her primary role was to make sure my constitutional rights were not violated – a very basic level of protection. But over our time together, I was surprised to find she not only cared, she did her job exceedingly well.

I remember sitting in her office during that first meeting as she asked me a bunch of questions about the case. I could tell she had studied whatever information was available, and was now trying to figure out my involvement. She wanted to know how I first came to invest in the company, so I told her about Wes.

"But how did you first meet *Lawrence?*" she asked, clarifying.

"I never met him," I explained. "I mean, I've talked to him on the phone a lot. But, I've never met the man." Not surprisingly, she was completely floored!

"What do you mean you've never met him?" she demanded, astonished. "How could you work for someone for more than a year and not have met him? It was not that big a company." I could sense the skepticism in her tone. She wondered what I was hiding, but I was telling the truth. To this day, I still have never met Lawrence face-to-face.

Even the FBI agents I spoke with later could not believe I'd never met Lawrence. Coopersmith, the prosecutor, eventually pulled out a picture of Lawrence from his driver's license record, and I didn't even recognize him. When Coopersmith told me that the picture was, in fact, Lawrence himself, I was stunned. I'd always imagined him to be a well-groomed businessman, wearing the expensive clothing, looking more than worthy of running a multi-billion-dollar company.

Simply told, he didn't look like that at all. He looked shockingly underwhelming. Honestly, I don't know how to describe what he looked like without offending a certain vocational group of people, so I won't try to paint you a picture. Suffice it to say, he did not look like he could own a highly successful company. Frankly, he didn't look like he could find his way out of a pool hall, let alone manage an IPO.

"Carol, he hired me over the telephone," I explained. "Every time Lawrence said he would come by my office, offering to take me to lunch or whatever, something would always come up. He would always cancel the meeting. When I would go to the company headquarters and ask for him, the front desk person would tell me he wasn't there. In fact, on one occasion, she actually said, 'Lawrence is like a ghost. He's almost never in his office.'"

Carol continued to drill me with questions, and in turn questioned every answer I offered. She made it clear that she did not believe me.

The process was grueling. She accused me on multiple occasions of holding back or not being forthright with her. I would get angry at her accusations, and sometimes end up in tears.

On one visit, she told me that her investigator spoke with my good friend Eric Sears, who had worked for me in IR. Carol said that Eric told the investigator I'd partnered with Lawrence, and was hiding millions of dollars in offshore bank accounts.

"That's not true!" I screamed. "I did no such thing, and Eric would never have lied like that. Your investigator is full of crap!"

I was furious and frightened at the same time. I knew Eric would never say that to anyone, because it *was not* true. Plus, Eric was a man of integrity and honesty. He would never make up a story like that! I started to wonder if I was trapped in a rigged system, bent on unjustly sending me to prison for a long time. I didn't know what to do.

Later, in a different meeting with Carol – the one where I first learned about blind spots as I described in chapter one – she confessed that Eric never claimed any such fact. All he said was that I was a man of high character and would never have stayed with the company had I known what was really going on. She explained that she needed to know the real truth before she could do her job properly in defending me, and she apologized for the pain and anxiety she'd caused.

At first, I was angry that she caused so much emotional turmoil, but I'm not one to hold a grudge. I resolved to get over it, and thankfully, the rest of our conversations were more pleasant. She did her best to get the best possible outcome at sentencing, and she really did do a good job.

WHISTLER

In a weird happenstance, Rachel and I happened to have a prepaid getaway planned for Valentine's Day at the Whistler Resort in British Columbia. We'd planned it all way back in the Fall. On one hand, the timing couldn't have been worse. On the other hand, we both desperately needed the diversion. Anyway, it was nonrefundable, so we packed the car and drove to Whistler.

We had reservations in Whistler Village, a quaint Swiss-like resort town nestled at the base of the ski runs. During those icy winter days, people would walk across the cobblestone streets, carrying their skis to and from the lifts. At night, the village came alive with people laughing and carrying on with their friends in the warm bars and friendly restaurants.

The first couple of weekend days were fun and relaxing. Exactly what we needed. Monday was a different story.

It was late morning. Rachel and I sat on a chair lift heading to the top of the mountain, and my cell phone rang. It was George.

"Hey, buddy. I'm on a chair lift with Rachel heading to the top of the mountain. What's going on?" I was expecting the call, as George was at a hearing to determine if the company would be placed in receivership, or allowed to continue its push to go public. This was considered a civil hearing, as opposed to a criminal proceeding, and George was there as a representative of Cascade Pointe.

"Oh, Kev. This is not a good day, buddy. I am so sorry to break this news to you on your romantic getaway."

"Oh no," I said, my heart sick with dread. "What?" Rachel looked up at me with worried eyes; she could tell from my tone that something was very wrong.

"Kev," he went on, nervous to deliver the news, "the judge just officially shut down the company. She assigned a receiver to account for and liquidate all the assets." His voice faded as he recounted the events, sinking into more despair. "It's over," he finally added. "It's all over."

"George, I don't understand," I protested, "Lawrence said his legal team would be there in full force to argue the case and provide the judge all the proof she needed. What happened?"

"They're here, Kevin. Extremely smart attorneys from a very prestigious firm in Los Angeles are all here. In fact, after both sides presented their arguments to the judge, one of Lawrence's attorneys stood up and held an envelope in his hand. He said to the judge, 'Your honor, in my hand is a certified check for $10 million. This is all the company needs to finish the audits and S1 paperwork to go public. I ask that you allow us to complete the process we set out to do so that everyone wins.'" He hesitated, as if trying to figure out what he was saying. "What's weird, Kev, is that before the attorney could even finish his last sentence, the judge slammed her gavel down on her bench and ordered the company into receivership. Everyone on the defense side was stunned. It was like she'd made up her mind before the hearing even started! Kev, I can't handle talking about this anymore. I'll talk to you later." With that comment, George hung up. I learned from him later that he had talked himself into a state of deep depression.

I, too, was stunned. My heart sank. I was crushed. I think we all knew the hearing would be futile – that Lawrence was everything the FBI said he was. But we were clinging to this last thread of hope. We wanted it to work. We needed any shred of hope we could muster, to not feel like we were idiots for blindly following a blatant con-artist.

I simply did not want to believe that Lawrence was nothing more than a criminal. To believe that would mean everything we'd fought for was a façade. It would mean that all my friends and family, including my father-in-law, would lose their hard-earned investments, and I would be to blame for introducing them to the opportunity. I felt like such a fool; I wanted anything to stem the rush of shame.

It would also mean Rachel was right when she told me she didn't have a good feeling about me taking the position. I hate it when she is right! I'll never live that one down.

Even after signing the plea bargain, both Rachel and I were not convinced I would actually serve time. We both believed that my cooperation with the government as a star witness would get me probation, possibly a fine.

That was the hope we clung to for the next two years.

CHAPTER SIX:

THE LONGEST TWO YEARS

After signing the plea bargain, I was allowed to remain out of prison on my own recognizance for just over two years. During that time, the government compiled its case and brought charges against the boss and ten other co-conspirators. I was not one of them. I was a leading witness helping the government with the case.

I didn't realize it at the time, but my original attorney did me a great favor when he found a way to get me assigned to a public defender. Since I had signed my plea bargain right away, I was never formally indicted by a grand jury.

Because I was never indicted, I was also never formally arrested or charged with a crime. The prosecutor and my attorney just negotiated a plea bargain: a legal contract where I would voluntarily accept my complicity and agree to serve up to a certain term in prison. The plea bargain itself contained the formal charges of one count of conspiracy to commit securities fraud, wire fraud, mail fraud, and money laundering, and one count of mail fraud. Each count bore a maximum of five years in prison.

Waiting for my sentencing was the longest two years of my life. I think it was even harder to deal with than the thirty-three months I finally did serve. I was in a constant state of limbo awaiting my sentencing hearing; I didn't know when the day would arrive to seal my fate. Everything was unknown – I just had to wait.

The government seized all our assets. They told us they would be selling our home, and that we should prepare to move out. My attorney said it would take time for them to get the paperwork in order. She would give us as much notice as possible. We ended up living there for nine more months. We did our best as a family to not dwell on the future. We loved each other and continued to try and live a normal life, but for Rachel and me the stress of not knowing was always painfully present. The kids did their best to just be kids; they went to school and had fun with their friends in the neighborhood.

Rachel did not work outside the home, and I was now looking for a job. Job hunting was extremely depressing. Though we didn't believe I would go to prison, we really didn't know what would happen at sentencing. The unknown made it incredibly difficult to look for anything that even vaguely resembled permanence.

I had a fantastic interview with a national company that provided supplies to restaurants. But by the time I got to the third interview, I felt obligated to share my situation with the general manager. He said he would need to run my situation up the proverbial flag pole and get back to me. The next day, he called to say he would love to hire me but was not allowed. He left the door open for me to contact him after sentencing, which of course would never have happened.

In the meantime, I answered an advertisement for a job as a bill collector. That was discouraging, but I was getting desperate. At this point, any job was better than no job. We were selling furniture just to get by; it was painfully humbling.

I showed up for my interview with Sam, the general manager of Credit International. This was a nationwide collection agency and check guarantee company that had been in business for 23 years, and ranked highly on the Nilson report, a trusted publication in the payments industry. While I was waiting in the lobby for Sam to escort me back to his office, a middle-aged man walked out of the back-office door into the lobby. It wasn't Sam. He stopped and looked at me. I looked at him. He had a friendly face and was very fit; had I seen him somewhere before?

His eyes finally lit up. "Oh, I remember you!" he said, nodding to himself. "We met at Starbucks earlier this year. Great to see you again! What are you doing here?"

"I'm meeting with Sam to interview for a collector position," I told him. "Do you work here?"

"Actually, I own the place. Great seeing you again! Sorry, though, I gotta go. I'm heading out to a meeting." He turned out the door, and I didn't think much of it.

Finally, Sam arrived, and brought me into his office. He could not have been more than 29 or 30 years old, and he was the collection manager. He looked over my job application and resume. We chatted briefly. Then he looked me square in the eyes and said, "Kevin, I can't hire you. You are over-qualified for the position. You will never earn the kind of income you have been used to earning over the last ten plus years."

"Sam, that's okay," I said, "It's not about how much I can earn. I just need a leg up. Any income is more than I have now... I've sort of fallen on hard times." I was gun-shy about bringing up any more details at this point, especially after my last interview.

Unfortunately, Sam could not be persuaded. I was escorted back out of the building.

I drove home even more depressed. "If I can't get a job as a bill collector," I thought to myself, "who will ever hire me?" No offense to bill collectors, of course, but the position is not exactly known for its tremendous longevity. "I suppose I could always go back to selling cars!" I thought bitterly. That idea only caused even more anxiety.

I went home and told Rachel what happened. As an after-thought, I added the part about running into Ron – what a strange coincidence, we agreed!

Then the phone rang.

SERENDIPITY

It was Ron, the owner of the company.

"Kevin, this is Ron Stevenson. Sam filled me in on your interview. Listen," he said, matter-of-fact, "I don't believe in co-incidences. Would you mind coming back to my office to meet with me?"

"Sure. When?" I was puzzled, but excited. Here was a possibility!

"How soon can you be here?"

"I'm on my way. Be there in 10 minutes."

I drove to his office, curious to see what he had in mind. There I was sitting in the lobby again, this time to see the own-er. I sat there for a couple minutes with great anticipation, but I was also a little guarded. I instinctively wanted to protect my-self from another letdown.

Ron came out and escorted me to his office. It was modest in size, and in a bit of disarray, with stacks of paperwork piled all over his desk. I sat in a chair directly across from him as he took his seat.

"I looked at your resume, Kevin, and I'm impressed," he said, not beating around the bush. "So, tell me: why are you applying for a lower level job as a bill collector?"

I appreciated Ron's no-nonsense style, and decided to share everything. As concisely as possible, I brought him up to speed.

He sat back in his chair, pondering my story for a minute. Finally, he said, "That's amazing, Kevin. I think the Lord has brought our paths together for a reason. I'd like to offer you a job, but," he added, "not as a bill collector. Right now, I need a good salesperson to help bring on new business accounts. I'll pay you a salary, plus commission, and show you what to do. You'll earn more than you would as a collector. But there's something else I want to share with you that might even be more important. Are you interested?"

"Wow!" I said, overwhelmed with gratitude. "Thank you, Ron. Of course, I'm interested in whatever you have to say."

"Great. When we met in Starbucks, I mentioned that I owned several businesses. This is just one of them. I also work with a group of very successful business people out of Spokane, Washington. They have become mentors to me and helped set me up in an online shopping business."

While he told me this story, my mind went back to a friend who, a couple of years ago, started telling me the same exact story. I had to interrupt him.

"Ron, are you talking about Quixtar (Amway's former online brand)?"

"Yes!" he said. "So, you *are* familiar with it?"

"I am. I've never really been interested in the Amway business. Not that I have anything against it. It just never seemed like my kind of business," I explained. "But please continue. I agree that we are not sitting here by accident!"

Ron continued, explaining that he and his wife, Sue, were leaders in the organization and derived a healthy six-figure income from their efforts. They had been involved for fifteen years.

"Listen," he said, finishing up his story, "the sales job is yours regardless of what you decide about Amway. But, if you would like me to mentor you, and help you create a residual income that might support your family in the event you actually have to leave for a while, I'm happy to do that as well."

I definitely needed mentorship from an honest businessman. Plus, I liked the idea of creating a back-up plan for my family, in case our wishful thinking about prison turned out to be wrong. So, I accepted both offers.

Over the next two years, I had three jobs. One was to drive around the greater Seattle area, knocking on business doors and looking for those in need of a collection agency. The second was to meet with potential recruits who might join the Amway business. Most of these meetings were in their homes, in the evenings. The third job, which was compulsory, was to meet with the prosecutors and/or my attorney whenever they said to meet. These meetings were always during the business day, but thankfully Ron was flexible and accommodating.

MY DAY JOB

My day job as a salesperson was daunting. I was dealing with so much emotional baggage that it was hard to carry on a lively conversation with a complete stranger about *their* financial collection needs. To make matters worse, every time I knocked on the door of a business to speak with the owner, I was paralyzed with fear that they would know me. If they weren't one of the actual 5,000 investors, they might have been following the case in the newspaper. Either way, I would not be someone they'd want to do business with.

This fear consumed me. Some days I just pulled over to the side of the road and wept. My emotions were fragile. I might have been on the brink of a nervous breakdown. One day, at home in the kitchen, I reached in the fridge to grab a milk carton. It slipped out of my hand and smashed against the kitchen floor, splashing milk everywhere. I started crying like a baby. I guess that's what they mean by "crying over spilled milk." Rachel cleaned up the mess and consoled me. I'm not sure what I would have done without her.

After working for Ron for about six months as a (failing) sales rep, he called me into his office.

"Kevin, I've been thinking. I think your talents are being wasted in the field. I have an idea. I've always wanted to create a "receivables guarantee" program, but I've never had the right guy to make it work. Maybe we could work on building this together? If you do have to go away for a while, this could provide an ongoing income for Rachel and the kids."

I was all ears!

Ron not only ran this national collection agency, he was the creator of the original "check guarantee program." Until debit cards took over, most merchants accepted checks. The problem was, of course, that some people would write checks when they didn't have enough money in their account – so the merchant would lose out. Their only recourse was to send the check to a collection agency in hopes they would recover a percentage of the face value.

Along came Ron, and his check guarantee program. He did the math and figured out how to guarantee the merchant that 100% of the checks they accepted from customers would be backed – he covered the risk himself. That is, if the merchant become a customer of CCV, Ron's check guarantee company, then CCV would reimburse the merchant for any check that did not clear the bank. Ron would then turn the check over to his collection agency, and they would pursue getting that money back from the maker. It was a brilliant idea that ultimately swept the nation.

With his knowledge of the check guarantee business, Ron always believed he could do the same guaranteeing receivables. For instance, most dentists allow their patients to make payments, but dentists run into the same problem. They're not able to collect a certain percentage of those debts. Enter Ron's concept of a receivables guarantee program.

I loved the idea! I loved the business concept itself, but even more I loved the chance to get out of selling collection services. Ron agreed to bring me on as a 50/50 partner in the business if it took off.

Together, we created E-Z Pay Solutions, a dental patient, receivables guarantee company. We chose to focus first on the dental industry, since dentists were notorious for accepting payments for treatment. Plus, a lot of published financial data was available. We planned to open up new markets in new industries later, after first getting some traction in this niche.

We laid a great foundation, developed the systems and processes, created the marketing materials, and away we went. I brought on several accounts right away; pretty soon we started growing and adding staff. It was a great diversion during the pre-trial period; most importantly, it provided hope for me and my family. I'll never forget George's words, *"You can cope when there's hope!"*

I continued to meet with potential Amway recruits, and Rachel helped a lot on that side of things. Whenever I would meet with a couple, she would go with me. Whenever we sold products, she would pick them up and help distribute them to customers or other independent business owners (IBO's). Despite her constant support, building the Amway business was a real struggle. It challenged my insecurities, and was emotionally draining. I didn't have much to offer as a mentor. We ultimately gave up on trying to earn an income with it. Still, to this day I have the utmost respect for the company and many of its products and people. Ron and his wife became great friends that stuck with us through everything; they remain our good friends today.

On top of building E-Z Pay *and* trying to build our Amway business, I was still driving downtown regularly to meet with the Assistant United States Prosecutor, Jeff Coopersmith, and Carol, my defense attorney.

WORKING WITH THE FEDS

Meeting with Coopersmith was surreal.

Each time, I would wait for Carol in the lobby of the prosecutor's office. We would then be escorted to a large boardroom, not unlike the fancy boardrooms you see in lawyers' offices on television. The conference table easily sat twelve people in cushy leather chairs.

Carol and I would take seats on one of the sides near the front. The prosecutor, Coopersmith, would come in and sit down at the head of the table. He wore a two-piece suit and open-collared dress shirt. He always came across as very intense and focused, with half a subtle smirk on his face like the cat that cornered the mouse. He was civil and professional, but there was no time (or desire) for small talk. As soon as everyone was there, we got right down to business. Usually, across from us sat Coopersmith's assistant, one or two of the FBI agents in charge of the investigation, and a representative from the IRS.

Coopersmith had several manila folders stacked in front of

him, and was loaded with questions as he tried to make sense of what the FBI later called the largest stock fraud case in the history of the State of Washington. My job was to answer his questions and to help him put the pieces of the puzzle together.

Most of these visits are a blur – a barrage of questions, sprinkled throughout with attempts to help them all make sense of the answers in view of what they believed to be true.

Every now and then my answers wouldn't satisfy Coopersmith's presupposition. He would accuse me of hiding something, or holding back. He was convinced I was in on the scam, and should therefore know more of what Lawrence was thinking and scheming. The problem was, I didn't know everything. That really frustrated him. To Coopersmith, the idea of someone being an unwitting accomplice, as Carol called me, was completely absurd.

He suffered from the Occupational Blind Spot.

OCCUPATIONAL BLIND SPOT

Occupational blind spots happen when your occupations become the center of your life and shape how you experience everything else. You begin to lose touch with the rest of the world. You begin to "believe your own press," as the saying goes. You no longer experience your occupation as just that: a job or career. Your occupation becomes *who you are*. It consumes you. It infiltrates your worldview.

In Coopersmith's case, as a result of the necessary skepticism in his profession, he had become hardened in judgment. By the time someone was meeting with him in his conference room, they were already guilty. That was what so much of his experience had taught him. Which meant, in his mind, that they could not possibly be good people with good intentions, who made bad choices. They had to be bad people, or, at the very least, good people with bad intentions. Which is how he treated me, and the others in the case.

I saw this blind spot a lot in real estate. Some top producers would become extremely arrogant; they would add all of their certifications behind their name and "strut their stuff" to fellow agents. It's one thing to be proud of your accomplishments. It's another thing to let your occupational success go to your head. Some were so consumed by their own accomplishments, they actually expected their *clients* to esteem them for it. You have probably never been impressed by the alphabet soup behind a real estate agent's name. Most consumers have no idea what those letters mean. Nor do they care! Some are even appalled by the arrogance. But when you're stuck behind the Occupational Blind Spot, you don't notice that sort of thing.

In my work now as a public speaker, author, trainer and coach, I recently spoke to an internal auditor and fraud examiner who, unwittingly, shared her own occupational blind spot.

While we were talking about her job, and in particular, one of her cases, she commented, "I've seen *everything* in my career. Nothing shocks me anymore. No one is innocent."

If she could only hear her own words. She has crossed the line from skepticism to cynicism.

Another example comes from the medical field. You've probably heard the phrase "god complex" attributed to some doctors. They're the ones who've become victims of the occupational blind spot. They might very well be amazing doctors; they might be on the top of their game and highly recognized within the medical field for their skills. But when they take on an attitude that the rest of us should bow down before them, or kiss the ground they walk on, you know they've lost touch.

It's natural to want to be validated. You want to be recognized for your accomplishments. That's normal. But when you lose touch with the rest of the world, you've become a victim of the occupational blind spot.

If you are secure in who you are as a person, your occupation is simply what you do, not who you are. The minute your occupation defines who you are, you have become a victim of the occupational blind spot.

> *Blind Spot Challenge: Is your identity and self-worth derived heavily from your occupation?*

TRANSCRIBING THE TAPES

Coopersmith eventually relented, and quit trying to force answers or put words in my mouth. But I'm not sure he ever changed his posture about my lack of knowledge of the crime. Fortunately, I was still helpful. Since I was very active in the investor community, I heard all the rumors and had a pretty good idea of who was doing what to help the company move forward. That information, along with my date- and time-stamped tape recordings, allowed him to piece together the timeline to build a solid case against Lawrence.

Coopersmith had the tapes transcribed, but they had a lot of trouble with the process. Even when significantly slowing down the playback speed, the transcribers had a hard time understanding what Lawrence was saying. Which meant I had a new job: to review all the transcripts against the tapes, and fix all the errors. It was tedious and exhausting.

I drove to Carol's office once or twice a week, and spent between two and four hours working on the transcripts. She set me up with a workstation, equipped with a large stack of transcripts and a cassette transcription machine – old-school style with a foot pedal to start and stop the playback. I read the transcript fastidiously while listening to the audio. If there was a mistake or missing section, I would press the foot pedal to stop the tape, then write in the correct wording.

Carol needed to be present as I worked on the transcripts, so between my work and her schedule, it took more than a month to complete

My assistance was greatly appreciated by the prosecutor. He told Carol that I was a model cooperating witness; later, he told the same to the judge when my sentencing day finally came.

SENTENCING DAY – FINALLY

The original sentencing date had been postponed at least four times. Each time, a new development in the case against Lawrence meant the prosecutor needed more help, so my own sentencing would be put off.

Once again, I was given a new sentencing date. This time for July 6, 2004.

Rachel and I were mentally preparing for the dreaded day when Carol called. We immediately assumed she was calling to postpone sentencing yet again; that's what we'd come to expect.

"Kevin, a big, unrelated case was won that could affect your sentencing," she said. "The case calls into question the legality and validity of the Federal Sentencing Guidelines. Judges from coast to coast are not sure how they should rule in their pending cases. If this case causes a reversal of the guidelines, it could mean the judge would have the freedom to give you probation or a light six-month sentence! But don't get your hopes up. No one knows for sure what this means."

"What does this mean for Tuesday?" I asked. I was excited, but still felt like we were in limbo.

"That's the other reason I'm calling," she explained. "I spoke with the clerk at the courthouse. She said that as of now, Judge Peckman is still planning on proceeding with your sentencing. But there is a high probability that it will get canceled once she reviews the other case more thoroughly. So, plan on showing up. But, expect to have it canceled."

Very clear instructions, as you can tell.

"Carol, this is so frustrating," I said. "I have a bunch of friends, relatives and pastors planning to attend the hearing as character witnesses. What am I supposed to tell them?" Carol had been prepping me for two years to bring as many character witnesses as possible to the sentencing hearing – a way to show the judge that I had people who knew me and believed in me. She even asked me to have them write letters. I did as she suggested; fifteen of them wrote glowing letters expressing their view of my character, asking the judge for lenience.

"Based on what other judges are doing throughout the country, I think there is a 90% chance your hearing will get canceled. So, you decide. But, if it was me, I might call everyone and tell them they don't need to show up."

"Okay," I said, dejected, "I'll think about it."

Rachel and I decided to tell her parents, my parents and all our friends and family to not bother showing up on Tuesday. Based on all the other cancelations and now this big news and Carol's 90% prediction, we didn't want to waste anyone's time. Big mistake!

Tuesday morning came, and there was no call from Carol to cancel the hearing. Rachel and I showed up on schedule. We parked the car and walked to the federal courthouse. After walking through a metal detector, we made our way down a long hallway lined with dark wood paneling, leading to the door to the courtroom.

On our left were several tiered rows of chairs for visitors. On the right was a short, wooded rail wall, with a double gate in the middle. Rachel took a seat in the visitors' section, while Carol summoned me to enter through the gates. She was sitting on a long table to my left, accompanied by her assistant. On the right was another long table, where Coopersmith and his assistant sat reviewing their paperwork.

There were only three other people in the courtroom: the bailiff, and the court reporter, stationed up front on each side of the judge's bench. The third was a thirty-something year old man, sitting behind my wife in the visitors' section. We didn't know who he was until later: the sole reporter from the Seattle P-I newspaper, assigned to track the progress of the case. He tried to ask Rachel questions but she refused. He didn't even bother with me.

That was it. Not one friend, not a single relative, no other people in the courtroom as character witnesses or for moral support. Why should they be? We'd told them not to come. I was furious at Carol. Ultimately, it was our choice to tell them to not come – but we had trusted her advice. This wasn't going to go well. To the judge, it looked like I had no one in my life who cared about me, other than my wife. Ugh.

The hearing didn't take long. The judge asked a few questions, and then wanted me to acknowledge that I did, in fact, sign the plea bargain. Then, she asked the prosecutor for his sentencing recommendation. He told her that I was a model witness, probably the most cooperative witness he'd ever worked with. With that, his recommendation was for me to serve forty-eight months.

Carol had prepared me for this ahead of time. Her plan was to counter with forty months.

It didn't work.

The judge made a shocking statement as a personal verbal attack, then slammed her gavel on the bench and ordered me to serve forty-eight months. I was to self-surrender to the federal prison in thirty days.

I looked back at Rachel. She looked horrified. We were stunned. Neither of us believed this would happen. Even when Carol prepped me, it had never quite sunk in that this was really happening.

To top it off, the judge was vicious and vindictive in her comments.

"Mr. McCarthy, I am greatly concerned about how you co-operated with the government in this case. If you could follow Lawrence as much as you did, then suddenly switch your loyalty and allegiance over to the government, I fear you have no moral center. I'm giving you forty-eight months to find your-self."

"No moral center!" I thought bitterly. *"Are you out of your mind?!"* I was furious. I looked at Carol and whispered, "Can I say something back to her?"

"I would keep your mouth shut. She can still increase your sentence."

So, I did. I kept my mouth shut. But I was shaking with in-dignation. I had already admitted I'd made a mistake; I knew there were consequences to that. But to be attacked because I'd been honest? To have my "moral center" questioned when I'd been trying so hard to do the right thing? The only reason I "jumped sides" was because it was the right thing to do. I'd found out my side was the wrong one, so I left it! Wasn't that the right thing to do? Once my eyes were opened, why wouldn't I cooperate? And *that* was what she blamed me for? This was crazy! I was steaming.

But I had to contain myself, or things could get worse.

As if her initial statement wasn't bad enough, when she passed the forty-eight-month sentencing judgment, she made another comment.

"I am going to see to it," she snapped, "that you don't even take up a collection of offerings in church!"

Seriously? I could barely handle it. Why the personal attacks? Carol had warned me that Peckman hated fraud. She was equivalent to the proverbial "hanging judge" when it came to fraud cases. But did she really need to say the things she said? Being pinned for a terrible mistake is bad enough; it's exponentially worse when your motives are attacked so heartlessly. While all this went through my mind, Judge Peckman filled out some paperwork. Coopersmith shuffled papers on his desk. Carol and I sat patiently for the bailiff to call, "all rise."

When he did, I quickly went over to Rachel. We embraced. She was still stiff with shock. I probably was, as well.

After an instructional debrief with Carol, Rachel and I left the building and drove home. We had to pull over on the way to come to our senses. She was angry, then upset. She cried, then we cried together.

"Certainly, this can't be the final answer," she said. "It's not God's answer. A miracle is still coming, and somehow, you'll be home in six months or less! I really believe that!"

"Me too," I replied. But I wasn't sure if I did. I wanted to believe I would receive probation, but it was a struggle. I really didn't know for sure. Still, I didn't want to shake Rachel's hope. She needed to cling to it even more than I did. *We can cope when there's hope!*

With that, we drove home silently, each of us deep in thought and prayer. We were both wondering how we would break the news to the kids that their dad was leaving for a while.

OUR CHILDREN

We have two children. Christopher (he prefers Chris) was thirteen, and Noelle was eleven. We sat them down on the couch and explained as best we could what had happened in the courtroom.

They had a difficult time processing the information, let alone understanding that I would be gone for a few years. We let them know we were hoping I would be home in six months or less, but I'm not sure it mattered. They could not comprehend the gravity of the situation. Chris had a hard time understanding how I could be going to prison when I wasn't the one who was committing the crime; it took him years to come to grips with that concept. Noelle just reached over and clung to me with a death grip, as if she refused to let me go. It brought tears to both our eyes; I didn't want to let her go, either.

As difficult as this was, I am happy to report that both of our young adults are doing well. We're proud of who they've become, and how they worked through missing their father during those crucial years of adolescence.

Knowing I would be leaving in about thirty days, we received some good counsel from our pastor. Even though we really couldn't afford it, we took a family vacation to build some memories before I left. We drove from Seattle to Pasadena, California, to attend a Christian conference, and go to Disneyland. Several family members from Phoenix met us there. It was a wonderful time.

When the trip was over and we returned to Seattle, Rachel and I attended a Mercy Me and Michael W. Smith concert on her birthday. Those memories gave me strength; four days later, she was dropping me off at the prison for my *self-surrender*.

CHAPTER SEVEN:

CLUB FED

SELF-SURRENDERING

The judge allowed me the dignity of self-surrendering to the federal prison. That meant I was free to leave the courthouse after sentencing, as long as I agreed to show up at the appointed time. I was given thirty-three days to report on August 9, 2004.

The morning of August 9th, Rachel and I drove four hours to the Sheridan Federal Correctional Institution. We were both at a loss for words on the drive. I had read a lot of information about Sheridan on a website, PrisonTalk.com; one of the things I learned was having visitors was not guaranteed. So, Rachel and I came up with a game plan. She would not plan to visit until she heard from me that it was okay. We both knew that could take up to two weeks.

We pulled into the parking lot and parked the car. I stepped out of the driver's seat. She slid behind the wheel, and I bent down to hug her. We sat there, holding each other, for what seemed like an eternity, but was probably only a couple minutes. Then she couldn't handle it any longer.

I gave her a kiss goodbye and closed her door. I started walking toward the double doors, the entry to the intake facility. As I took a few steps, I turned to watch Rachel go. She didn't look back. All I could see was the car rushing out of the parking lot.

She later told me she cried all the way to Portland. She didn't feel like she could make the drive back to Seattle, so she called a girlfriend from college and slept at her house for the night. That breaks my heart.

I walked up to the counter where a uniformed officer – a prison guard – was sitting. I told him who I was, and that I had an appointment. He had me sit in a chair in the lobby and wait for someone to escort me behind the locked, steel door behind him.

A few minutes later, that door opened with the sound of a buzzer. A different guard called my name.

I got up and walked towards him. He escorted me through a series of doors, each unlocked one at a time, only after the previous door securely locked.

He left me in a holding room. I suppose it was a cell of sorts, with a cement bench that doubled as a bed. There was a toilet and a sink. Nothing else. He didn't close or lock the door – he just left. Not knowing what else to do, I sat.

I lost track of time. It was a couple hours later when a woman in civilian clothes came to the room and called me out. She was my assigned counselor, Ms. Daniels. I later learned that she had an office in the dorm where I would be assigned. That struck me as odd – that the prison would have female counselors, with offices inside the sleeping quarters of a male prison.

Daniels filled out a stack of papers for my intake interview. She was tall, conservatively-dressed, in her mid-forties. Her shirt collar went up to her chin, and her skirt went to the floor. She was professional and cordial, but she also made it clear she had no interest in developing a personal relationship. Even though her title was counselor, it felt more like she was just an administrator.

The intake interview took about an hour. Daniels reviewed my case file, and asked a slew of questions, all to help her better understand the person she would be dealing with for the next four years.

As she finished her last form, she placed it back in the brown folder with my name on it.

"Follow me," she said, standing abruptly. "I'll show you were the laundry unit is so you can get your bedroll." The bedroll consisted of two sheets, one military style wool blanket – which reminded me of the Air Force – and a lumpy, flat pillow.

We walked across the street from the high security prison and intake facility to the laundry unit, located in the minimal security camp. I picked up my bedroll and walked outside. Daniels pointed me to the dorm directly across from the laundry, then walked back to the administration building.

"The Camp," as my facility came to be known, housed first-time offenders with non-violent crimes. Unlike the high security prison, with its double chain-link fence covered with rolls of razor-wire, the camp only had a single straight fence behind the buildings. That fence, which separated the prison property from a public park, was more to keep the locals out than to keep the inmates in.

Since the camp was not completely fenced, Daniels pointed out where the other boundaries were: a road winding through the prison property on one side, a building on another, and a field where crops grew in season on the other.

THE DORMS

There were five buildings in the camp, two of which were large dormitories capable of housing 256 men each. At one point, there was a total of 504 men in the camp, but of course that number fluctuated slightly over my thirty-three months.

The dorm had one main entrance in the middle of the front side of the building. It opened into a large foyer, and as you first entered, you'd see two wide winding staircases directly in front of you. One led to the second floor on the left, and the other to the second floor on the right.

On each side of the staircases on the first floor were small countertops, upon which sat commercial grade microwaves. The men were allowed to use the microwaves at will to heat water or cook food – but more on that later.

To the left and right of the foyer on both floors were short hallways, or "wings" as we called them, leading to the dorm laundry rooms and the sleeping quarters. The inmates had a choice for laundry: they could either drop off their clothes each week to the laundry facility, and pick them up the next day, or they could wash them themselves in the dorm laundry room. The camp laundry service was free, but the dorm laundry required you to purchase laundry soap from the commissary.

Each dorm also had three television rooms. Each room had between fifteen and twenty chairs, with one thirty-six-inch television mounted on a shelf on the wall. Each of these rooms had only one remote control. "Yikes!" I thought. "Don't these people know about men and their remote controls? Well, at least these are chairs and not recliners, or we'd really have problems."

Actually, the television rooms *were* the scene of the few fights that happened while I was there. They might not have been recliners, but those chairs were important. The first time I decided to watch a television program, I entered one of the rooms. It was empty, so I turned on the TV and took a seat in the middle of the room. Ten minutes later, another guy walked in. He walked right up to me, looked down, and said, "Hey buddy, that's my chair."

Puzzled, I looked around the room at the many, many empty chairs. Then I looked back up at him, nervous, and said, "Uh, there's lots of other chairs…"

"I know. But you're in *my* chair. Get up!" Was this guy for real? I started wondering if I should call him Bubba.

By his facial expression, I could tell that he was not in a joking mood. So, quietly and politely, I got up from his seat and moved to the back row. He promptly sat down without incident.

Later I learned that there was a pecking order, based mostly on seniority. Guys would claim ownership of a chair, and when they wanted to sit in it, they did. Even though it was against prison policy, the guys respected this system. When an inmate who "owned" a chair left the prison, he would usually gift his chair to a buddy. I eventually had my own chair gifted to me. Yes, there were even a few times when I asked someone to get up. I relied on peer pressure from the rest of the guys to motivate the squatter to move, and it worked. Those who know me know I asked nicely – I didn't have many options. Let's just say I certainly didn't look like a Bubba!

When it came to watching certain TV programs, the majority always ruled, except for NASCAR days. When NASCAR started all other programming stopped, even if there was only one NASCAR fan in the room. Let me tell you, I learned to seriously appreciate fast cars driving around in circles for hours on end. I still avoid left turns when I drive!

In one of the wings, instead of a television, there was a tiny library just large enough for several well-stocked bookcases. The books were all used, placed there by inmates. We were allowed to receive books in the mail as long as they were shipped directly from the publishers or bookstores. I suppose the prison didn't want the proverbial file-embedded-in-a-book sent from home.

Another wing had a larger library, which after hours doubled as an unofficial poker room. Of course, gambling is strictly against the rules, but that didn't stop the dedicated players. They would send a stakeout to the end of the hall to keep an eye out for incoming guards. If they got the signal, the card players would hide their chips as quickly as possible. The chips were actually just postage stamps, with a face value of thirty-six cents. To keep the math simple, though, each stamp was only worth thirty cents on the table, or for other internal commerce, which I'll explain later. Then it would appear to the guard to be just a friendly game. And that was the *real* game, because the guards always knew the guys were gambling. But as long as the guard didn't see any evidence, they'd turn a blind eye and move on. The term was to keep what we were doing off "Front Street."

Even though I enjoy a good game of Texas Hold'em, I resisted the urge to join in. Pool was a different story. One wing in each building had a room dedicated to a pool table. "Seriously?" I thought. "A pool table?" At least there was one bright spot in this otherwise dismal circumstance. Playing pool has always been a fun pastime, and in prison it became a place to escape the reality of being confined, if only for a few hours a week.

THE COMMISSARY

Outside the main building was a courtyard, adorned with lush grass, groomed trees, manicured shrubs and flowers. It did not strike me at all like what I imagined prison would look like. It felt more like a community college campus, except once you enrolled, you couldn't leave the campus until graduation!

Around this oasis were several buildings, the largest of which sprawled the length of both dormitories. Inside that enormous building was the most popular space of all: the commissary.

The commissary was where, if you had the means, you could purchase food and personal items. I was blessed that my parents would send me a couple hundred dollars a month, whenever they could, and that made a huge difference. Of course, I also earned money working in the prison, but I'll explain that later. We never saw the actual currency, since money was not allowed inside the camp. Instead, each inmate had a bank account managed by the prison staff. They kept a running balance of how much money we had, which we could then use to purchase items or make phone calls.

Each inmate was assigned one of the three commissary days to shop (Tuesday, Wednesday, or Thursday). We'd fill out our order form – or 'shopping list' – stand in line on our shopping day, and when it was our turn at the window, we'd turn that list in to the inmate manning the store. On the other side of the glass, this inmate would run around the stock room filling our orders before dumping all the requested goods through a drop shoot that opened to a collection bin. We then took our goods from the bin and loaded them in our commissary bags (which were also our laundry bags).

In the life of an inmate, there are few things as exciting as commissary day! Because I had the means, I was able to purchase food items to make my own meals in the microwaves back at the dorms – always better than the food provided. I bought: refried beans, tortillas, salsa, tuna and salmon sold in pouches, even ice cream. There were nearly two hundred options in all. We could also purchase non-food items such as AM/FM radios, headphones, tennis shoes, and basic clothing. Even though the prison provided some of these necessities, the quality was much better at the commissary.

Tuna was a main staple, if you could afford it. We made all kinds of meals using the ingredients from the commissary. Sometimes, we even added ingredients that came from the kitchen – 'out the back door' as they say. Much like the poker room, the guards knew the black-market ecosystem existed. They knew we took food from the kitchens. For the most part, as long as you didn't put it out on Front Street, they just turned a blind eye.

For the most part.

That first weekend, someone gave me a bag of microwave popcorn. So, my very first Saturday morning, after eating breakfast in the cafeteria, I filled a small plastic drinking cup with butter from the breakfast bar. I intended to add it to my popcorn, thinking myself clever. With the little cup in my hand in front of my body, I walked out the door and ran right into the Lieutenant. Remember how I said most guards would turn a blind eye? Well, that was not the case with the Lieutenant or senior staff.

He took one look at the cup and asked me what I was doing. I explained. He, however, failed to see the brilliance in my plan, and told me to follow him. He marched me to the kitchen staff office, "the kitchen cop," the inmates called him. After the Lieutenant explained the situation to the kitchen cop, he informed me I'd be called back to the kitchen after dinner to have my punishment doled out.

I was nervous the rest of the day. What kind of punishment would they implement? Was the kitchen cop someone I should be frightened of? I didn't know what to expect. But, in the end, I never got the call. I guess that was a warning. It worked. I *never* innocently walked out the front door with butter in my hand again. Definitely not. I discovered there were much more efficient ways to obtain butter. All you had to do was give certain inmates a postage stamp or two, and you could get most any ingredient you'd ever need for cooking on the black market.

CHEESECAKE FACTORY?

As I said before, my parents sent me money each month, and I also managed to earn some working in the prison. I did that by providing something no one else in the camp could provide: cheesecake.

Once an entrepreneur, always an entrepreneur, I suppose.

Using ingredients from the kitchen and the commissary, I figured out how to make cheesecake in the prison microwaves to sell to other inmates. I would purchase the cream cheese and vanilla wafers, for the crust, from the commissary. I would then buy sugar and butter on the black market from the kitchen guys.

Of course, we didn't have much to compare it to, but the cheesecake I made was pretty good (if I do say so myself). I mastered the art of baking those treats; I even came up with gourmet flavors by adding chunks of Snickers bars, bananas or strawberries. The guys would pay one book of stamps (which contained twenty stamps) for a regular eight-inch cheesecake, and two books for a gourmet cheesecake. I sold between eight and fifteen every weekend.

I would spend all morning on Friday or Saturday making cheesecake. I started with Tupperware-style eight-inch round plastic bowls with lids, which I got at the commissary. I lined them with the vanilla wafer crust, then added the cheesecake filling and let them cool all day to set. After dinner, the guys would come by my cubicle to pick up their pre-ordered cheesecake. I would also hand-deliver cheesecakes to my VIP customers, who were usually in the TV room anxiously waiting for their dessert to show up in time for movie night. It was a win-win business! I kept a bunch of guys happy by supplying a quality product, and they afforded me the ability to shop at the commissary.

Of course, I couldn't simply cash in the stamps to spend in the commissary. The cheesecake business was no different from the poker room. If I kept it off Front Street, everything worked out. So, instead of paying me in stamps, I asked the customers to purchase items on a shopping list equivalent to the one or two books of stamps they owed me. It worked out nicely.

When I left after thirty-three months, I actually sold my thriving cheesecake business to another guy who was not getting out for another year. He paid me to learn the ropes, and to meet my clients.

TURNING A BLIND EYE

You might be thinking that participating in the black market was not ethical. But, is it? How can you know that it is or isn't? I certainly could have eaten each meal in the cafeteria, and worn prison-issue clothes, right? But this was the choice I made to bring a little extra comfort to an otherwise difficult situation. If you apply the Utilitarian Approach to ethical decision-making, then you would weigh the "greatest benefit over harm for the majority of people."[35] Would it be safe to say that more people benefited from the cheesecakes than were harmed by the missing butter and sugar? Maybe. Either way, looking back at it all: I'm still glad I made cheesecakes.

What's more interesting is when the guards continually turned a blind eye to the obvious black-market activities, they empowered the black-market system to exist. By doing so, they

---

[35] *What is the Utilitarian approach?* Retrieved from
https://www.reference.com/world-view/utilitarian-approach-d8ea0dde7156dd84

embolden the 'unethical' behaviors from the inmates. This was another case of good people making bad choices due to ethical fading.

This is not to pass the blame from the decision-maker to the enabler – from the inmate, to the guard. It's simply to point out that both parties are contributing to the unethical behaviors in the organization.

This reminds me of the story about the lawyer. A client came in asking for a review of an important contract. The lawyer looked it over, asked a few questions, and made some suggestions. The client thanked him for his advice, and asked about the fee. The lawyer said, "That will be $100." The client pulled out his wallet, handed the lawyer a crisp $100 bill, and left. Later, the lawyer discovered that it was actually TWO $100 bills stuck together. Now he has an ethical dilemma. Does he tell his partner?

Leaders set the tone for the rest of the company. They must be beyond reproach if the company is to have an ethical culture.

The Barber Shop

Another service available in the same building as the commissary was the barber shop. There, we could walk in whenever it was open and get a free haircut. Although, for those who had the means, it was customary to give the barber a pouch of tuna as a tip. It was smart, too; tuna is a small price to pay to make sure you didn't end up accidentally bald.

The barbers were inmates. None of the barbers I knew had ever cut hair as a profession; they learned how through the old-fashioned apprenticeship. If an inmate had an interest in cutting hair (mostly for earning tips), all he had to do was offer to learn, and one of the other guys would teach him. They were always eager to teach; it was hard to find new recruits.

The Computer Lab

Further down the corridor was the laundry facility, where I first picked up my bedroll. Down from that and past the cafeteria (which was the largest room in the building) was a modest but modern computer lab. It was just large enough to accommodate sixteen workstations and the education officer's desk.

The computer lab offered classes in Microsoft Office products, such as Word or Excel. You had to apply for a seat in class, and only fifteen inmates were accepted at a time. It was a privilege, so the guys were always thankful for the opportunity. We learned through the use of computers and workbooks; if you needed to print, you could do so, provided, of course, the guard who ran the classroom checked it over to make sure it looked legit.

In order to print a document, the footer of each page needed to include the name and purpose of that document. For instance, if it was for a college correspondence course, then the footer would say as much. Now, the guard didn't seem to actually care whether or not the footer was accurate; as long as she saw information there. Some inmates took advantage of this opportunity to print business plans and manuscripts, neither of which were officially allowed.

The prison did not want inmates working on business plans or writing books while in custody. I suppose it makes some sense, although I did occasionally overhear inmates scheming their next caper and how to avoid getting caught. Those conversations always struck me as funny: people who have been caught asking other people who have been caught how to not get caught.

The Game Room

Next to the computer lab were the game, exercise, and music rooms, all combined under one main entrance. Inside the main room you'd find two ping-pong tables and a few pieces of cardio equipment. Off of that room was a space with a piano, a sound mixing board, an amplifier, speakers, and a few other instruments. I was amazed at all the musical talent available; I even had a chance to take piano lessons! Although Mitch had been arrested on a federal drug sting, he was a concert pianist, and simply masterful on the keys. We would meet three mornings each week for lessons.

Once I learned the basics, I joined one of several bands that alternated using the music room for practice. I'd learned just enough to play the chords to the songs, which was a nice mental escape.

The Cafeteria

The largest room in the building was the cafeteria; it had dozens of tables that sat up to four inmates each. The "chow hall" was open for breakfast from 5:30 to 7:30, lunch from 11:30 to 1:00, and dinner from 4:30 to whenever they locked the doors. Breakfast and lunch crowds varied based on the individual's working hours, but everyone ate dinner at the same time. They had to: dinner always came right after the four o'clock stand up count.

Counting Heads

Around 3:15 or 3:30 every day, the four o'clock *stand-up count* bell, as it was known, would ring throughout the camp. At that sound, no matter where you were, you were obliged to make your way back to your bunk in the dorm and wait for the guards to walk by as they counted everyone. If you missed it, you risked serious punishment.

There were other counts throughout the night: 9:00 pm, midnight, 3:00 am and 5:00 am (and a 10:00 am count on weekends). But the four o'clock was the most formal count of the day. It was the only one where we were required to stand up in front of our bunks. Before the guards arrived, most of the guys would mill around the dorm, loud and raucous. But as soon as anyone saw the guards start walking down the sidewalk, they would holler, and everyone would scurry back to their bunks.

POOL ROOM JUNKIES

On one particular occasion, my friend Mohammed and I were playing pool when the bell rang. We were having such a good time that we just kept playing. One of the guys came and warned us the guards were getting close; we looked out the window and saw them walking through one of the lower level wings. We knew that area would take them at least ten minutes to count, and we only needed about five to finish our game. So, we kept playing.

I was right in the middle of the shot that might have won the game, when through the open window someone yelled, "Busted!" It was one of the two guards. He'd snuck up on us by running around the outside of the building.

"You men bring me your ID cards, now!" he ordered, not at all pleased that we were playing pool, but a little too excited (in my opinion) at catching us red-handed.

"But, but…" Mohammed started to say – but then stopped. There was no point. The guard looked at us perplexed and said, "Apparently you thought *you* could see *us* but we couldn't see *you?*"

We just handed him our prison-issued ID cards, and he

told us to return to our bunks for count, after which we would supposedly be called to the admin building.

When count was over we met in the foyer, waiting for the officer to call. It didn't happen. The only announcement we heard came to call our building to chow. We went with them and proceeded to eat, and that's when the announcement came.

"McCarthy, Mohammed to the admin building," came the voice over the loud speaker. This was nerve-racking; most of the inmates who were called to the admin building didn't return for several days, even months. That was when you were sent off to solitary confinement at the SHU or Special Housing Unit, a.k.a. "the hole." I had not been sent to the hole, and was hoping this wouldn't be a first!

We thought for sure we'd be spending at least a day or two in the SHU.

As we entered the admin building, Officer Howard waited for us in his white, clean-pressed uniform. Most of the guys respected Howard because he was fair; he treated everyone with dignity. Unlike some of the guards, who often treated inmates like sub-human pond scum, Howard never judged anyone for being in prison. He remained professional and courteous, but could be stern when needed. He never had to be a jerk to get the guys do to exactly as he asked – we respected him that much.

Howard looked at Mohammed and asked him why he was playing pool during the stand-up count. Mohammed provided plenty of excuses.

"I didn't have my watch on. And, um, we were being kind of loud, and, umm, couldn't hear the bell. And..." Mohammed would have continued frantically, trying to find an excuse that would appease Howard, but he was cut off. Howard then looked at me.

"So, McCarthy, what's your excuse?"

I steeled myself. "Howard," I said, "I have no excuse. I apologize for being there during count. I didn't mean to disrespect you or your staff. It won't happen again." I just didn't see any benefit in making excuses. There was no really good reason for us to have been there; we just made a bad choice.

Howard paused, processing what we'd said. Then, finally, "Okay. Here's your punishment. Tonight, I want both of you to empty all the trashcans throughout both dormitories before you go to bed. Got it?"

"Okay, no problem!" Mohammed replied, delighted.

"Yes, sir!" I agreed, thrilled not to be going in the hole.

Mohammed and I turned to walk out the door when Howard called me back. "McCarthy!" he yelled. "Hang on. Come back here." Mohammed and I both turned back. "Not you, Mohammed," Howard snapped. "Get started on the trash, now!"

As soon as the door closed behind Mohammad, Howard turned to me. "McCarthy, I appreciate you owning your mistake and not giving me a bunch of lame excuses. You're off the hook. Let Mohammed empty the trash by himself. You're dismissed."

I couldn't believe it! At first, I chuckled under my breath. No punishment! But when I went back to the dorm and saw Mohammed emptying a trash can, I just didn't have the heart to let him do it alone. I started emptying the cans in the other wings. Together, it only took a couple of hours. I never did tell Mohammed the end of that story.

THE LEADERSHIP BLIND SPOT

The Leadership Blind Spot happens when you are oblivious to how much you lean on the power of your position or title to get things done. Those who follow you do so out of obligation, not respect. You are an *unaware* positional leader.

POSITIONAL LEADERS

There are two types of leaders: Positional and Earned. Officer Howard was a great example of an earned leader.

As the leadership expert Glenn Lopis wrote in *Forbes*, "Being the leader doesn't mean that you have earned respect. Too many leaders take their titles and authority for granted. Some leaders believe that they are owed and/or command some level of (unearned) respect just because of where they are positioned on the organizational chart."[36]

Positional leaders feel the need to leverage their titles and authority to get people to follow them, but they have not yet earned the respect they desire. If someone is new to leadership, then positional leadership is all they have; it's normal, even expected, for a certain period of time. But when that person has been in leadership for a while, they should be able to move from a positional leader to an earned leader. Sadly, in many organizations there are still far too many veteran leaders who are still merely positional. What does that look like, exactly?

---

[36] Llopis, Glenn (2013, Jul 22). *5 ways leaders earn respect from their employees.* Retrieved from http://www.forbes.com/sites/glennllopis/2013/07/22/5-ways-leaders-earn-respect-from-their-employees/amp/

Positional leaders who have not earned the respect and admiration of others are not very self-aware, although most believe they are. The research I cited earlier applies here, too: "According to a series of surveys by psychologist Tasha Eurich, outlined in her book, *Insight*, says that 95% of people think they are self-aware, but only 10-15% truly are."[37]

Because positional leaders are not aware of their lack of growth – a significant blind spot – they continue to demand respect from others. They place a lot of stock in the positions they have achieved and expect others to admire them accordingly. They expect others to esteem them purely because of the position they hold. These leaders can become narcissistic and arrogant; they tend to place a higher value on talent and expertise than they do on people skills. After all, they believe that people skills should come naturally, that relationships happen magically based on your rank. Therefore, within the corporate setting, they place little to no value on soft skills training. They see it as a waste of time and resources, the lowest of all priorities, at best; at worst, it's a training they openly mock.

Positional leaders turn to politics in order to move up the ranks. Since they are not aware of the need for genuine personal growth, they resort to manipulation and game-playing to succeed. They have no real influence. Their identity is wrapped up in their position. The moment they lose their title, they lose their identity, which can result in a direct hit to their self-esteem. They will scramble to get it back by seeking to reestablish a place of authority. Unfortunately, because they have not invested in genuine relationships, that personal battle is often a lonely one.

Prolific author and renowned speaker John C. Maxwell

---

[37] Kauflin, Jeff (2017, May 10). *Only 15% of people are self-aware - - here's how to change.* Retrieved from
https://www.forbes.com/sites/jeffkauflin/2017/05/10/only-15-of-people-are-self-aware-heres-how-to-change/#1aed835c2b8c

writes, "Position is the lowest form of leadership – the entry level. The only influence a positional leader has is that which comes with the job title. Positional leadership is based on the rights granted by the position and title. Nothing is wrong with having a leadership position. Everything is wrong with using position to get people to follow you. Position is a poor substitute for influence."[38]

A positional leader who never becomes an earned leader never reaches their full potential. Politics will only take them so far. Eventually, someone with more political savvy will outplay and displace them.

Completely unaware, the positional leader suffers from the Leadership Blind Spot.

EARNED LEADERS

Earned leaders, on the other hand, serve and invest in the lives of others. They are constantly looking for ways to improve their own people skills, as well as develop the skills of others. They genuinely care about people, and that care earns respect from their peers and followers. Earned leaders value people over process. While talent, expertise and process are still essential to the success of any organization, the earned leader recognizes the importance of developing leaders and building strong, sincere relationships. People willingly and whole-heartedly follow earned leaders because they *want* to, not because they have to. In the words of the great author, salesman and motivational speaker, Zig Ziglar (1926 – 2012), earned leaders believe they can "have everything in life they want if they will just help other people get what they want." [39]

---

[38] How Successful People Lead. John C. Maxwell, Center Street Hachette Book Group, Page 5
[39] Retrieved from
https://www.brainyquote.com/quotes/quotes/z/zigziglar381984.html

Have you earned the respect of your peers, and the followers you desire? What can you do to start moving from a positional leader to an earned leader?

THE GODFATHER

But back to prison. Remember the game room? Well, right next to that room was an outdoor space we called the "weight pile." It was a blacktop slab, approximately seventy-five feet long and fifty feet wide, covered by a metal roof. The only wall was the end of the building to which it was connected. Out there, we had a variety of weight lifting equipment, from free weights to universal machines. Though it was usually pretty busy during the early morning or late afternoon, only about ten percent of the men actually used the equipment. I suppose it's not much different from a fitness center; most of the members who join in January never show up after February.

If they were interested, inmates had the ability to earn a Certified Personal Trainer certification from a nationally recognized organization. I met such a man early in my sentence, who I warmly referred to as the Godfather. His name was Joe. Joe was finishing up a twenty-year sentence which started "behind the fence", that is, in the medium-high security prison. He worked his way into the minimum-security camp based on good behavior.

Joe was a great example of an earned leader. Of course, in his former years as a drug lord, he was a positional leader. No one wanted to mess with him. But early in his sentence, Joe committed to following Jesus Christ, and his life was completely turned around. By the time I met him, Joe was (and still is) the kindest, most thoughtful man I know. Everyone in the camp respected him, largely because of who he had become. He would be the first guy to help someone in need. He sought opportunities to mentor younger inmates and help them change their lives. If a guy didn't have money on their books to buy their own food or supplies, Joe would usually take care of them. Of course, his old reputation remained with him.

The guys who knew him the longest continued to respect him in part because of the old Joe they remembered.

I was introduced to Joe about two weeks into my stay. Since we were both Christians, and probably because of the deer-in-the-headlights look on my face, he took me under his wing. I became another one of his mentorship cases.

As I mentioned before, Joe was a certified personal trainer, so he regularly took me and two other guys to the weight pile. Rachel reminds me that when I left prison in 2007 I was her ironman, thanks to those weights. Today, well, I'm more like her Pillsbury Dough Boy.

In addition to the weight pile, we had a quarter-mile outdoor track that surrounded a football/soccer field. When Joe and I weren't lifting weights, we were speed-walking around the track. We would walk and talk, stopping every half-lap to use the pull-up bars. The exercise was just a fringe benefit; our discussions as we walked were rich with dreams, reflection, philosophy, personal growth, laughter, and sometimes even tears, although we'd never let anyone see us cry.

Being mentored by Joe had other benefits. He introduced me to the guys as his "new best friend." That was a secret code for, "give him the same respect." When I crossed paths with those men again, they called me "Mr. McCarthy."

Joe had the only seat in all the television rooms that also came with a square card table. No one used it to play cards. Occasionally a guy would put his foot up on it or eat on it while watching TV, but it was Joe's table, and everyone who entered the TV room knew it. Joe would eat there, or put his feet up during the race. Personally, I didn't spend much time watching television, but I did occasionally enjoy the weekend evening movies. So, one day, Joe told me (loudly and in front of the guys), "Hey kid, when I'm not sitting in this seat, it's yours!" Since Joe only sat in the TV room to watch NASCAR once a week, I had free access to the chair and table. It was great! That's how I acquired a seat of my own in the TV room.

I realize that some of these things – little perks like the chair in the TV room – may sound silly. What does it matter, really? But when your world is confined to a federal prison, every little perk makes life just a little easier. They feel like a big deal.

Joe left nine months before I did. I kept the chair and the table, and he moved home with his aging mother in southern California to take care of her. We've stayed in touch, and I'm happy to report that, aside from a few ailments of old age, he is doing well. He even found his soul mate.

MAIL CALL

Something else that made life easier was mail call. Every week-day afternoon, right after the stand-up count, one of the staff counselors would start calling out names as he reached into the mailbag. Hearing your name brought a rush of emotions. We would excitedly rush through the crowd to grab our letter, magazine, or package. Even junk mail was a pleasant treat!

With very few exceptions, I wrote to Rachel every day. She kept most of the letters, and wrote back as often as she could. Mail call on those days was absolute bliss!

CHAPEL

Directly across from the weight pile was a stand-alone building: The Chapel. It was universally available to any and all religious and spiritual groups, from Christianity, Judaism and Islam, to Universalism and the Rastafarians.

You entered the chapel into a large foyer. To the right was a library, with bookshelves on all four walls, and in the center, was a conference table with eight chairs. It was open to anyone who wanted to find a quiet place to study or meditate, stocked with books covering a wide range of religious topics.

To the left, there was a small office for the chapel clerk. It had a desk with one business style chair on one side, and two visitors' chairs on the other, where inmates could visit. The clerk's main job was to hand out Hallmark greeting cards upon request. They were donated to the prison, and provided the guys with an opportunity to send cards to their loved ones for birthdays, anniversaries, and major holidays. The clerk also had a video player and small television where you could watch self-help videos from the library. Some guys would just hang out with the clerk and talk.

Straight through the foyer and a set of double doors was the sanctuary. It contained a pulpit, an upright piano and fifty chairs. Christian services were held on Sundays. A variety of other services were held at different times for different groups.

When the chapel was empty, which was most weekdays, I would spend some time playing the piano to practice my lessons. There were moments in the chapel that were magical, not just for me, but for an inmate named Ira. When Ira saw me playing the piano, he would come in and ask me to play his favorite Christian worship song: "Above All." He said it took him back to a place with his wife. We never really spent much time together outside of those moments; Ira pretty much kept to himself. But I always think of him when I play that song, and wonder how he and his wife are getting along. We had such a special connection in those moments, and I can only hope he's doing well.

The chaplain was a staff person. He would only preside over the Catholic services, his personally claimed faith, but he also showed up on occasion and sat in his office. The rest of the Chapel operations were handled by Adam Green, an inmate who was finishing a twenty-two-year sentence. His job was to staff the chapel, make sure the facility looked great, and keep all operations running smoothly. I worked for Adam as a chapel clerk about nine hours per week, and on top of that I ended up spending most of my free time in the chapel library asking some very difficult questions.

THE ROAD LESS TRAVELED

One would think that being imprisoned would be a wake-up call, an opportunity to make changes in one's character. A place to shift perspectives to avoid making the same mistakes twice. Sadly, for many who face it, prison just isn't enough of a game-changer.

Over time, I noticed a pattern as new guys would join us at the camp. It seemed they metaphorically chose one of two paths. To borrow from Scott M. Peck's book by the same title, some of the guys took *the road less traveled*; other guys took the wide road. The more popular road.

The wide road led to sameness. It led to being comfortable, never challenged enough to grow. Just about anything was available for those on the wide road. The guys on this road would find other guys just like them. They could party, play poker, indulge in television, raise a raucous in the yard. In essence, they could simulate the life they had on the outside. The idea of self-improvement was foreign to them. These are the guys who run up the high rates of recidivism.

The road less traveled led to change. A smaller percentage of guys chose this path. They avoided associating with the party crowd. They were intentional about creating new relationships with others who were also on a journey of personal growth. Sometimes, cutting ties with those you're used to spending time with is an important step to personal change.

Some of the guys understood that. Most didn't.

CHAPTER EIGHT: WELCOME TO THE BLIND SPOT ZONE™

THE MINDSET CHALLENGE

Once acclimated to this new life, I began asking very diffi-cult questions as I sat in the chapel library. I started with the obvious: "How did I get here?" And, it's ever-present part-ner, "What *was* I thinking?!" You may be baffled as you read my story. I was baffled, too. How could I have believed and followed Lawrence. How could I have been so duped? The judge said I should have been smart enough to know what was going on. How could that be true when I felt so oblivious? I needed to know, but the idea of discovering flaws in my own reality terrified me.

In fact, if I was so duped by Lawrence, what other beliefs did I hold that might be just as wrong? What about my belief in Christianity? Could the whole thing be a farce? I wondered if this is what insanity looked like. Welcome to the BlindSpot Zone™.

The mission was to discover the answers. I had discovered the concept of biases and perspectives. So, I knew I had to do my best to set my biases aside. It's impossible to be completely unbiased, but at least I could maintain awareness, and try to keep the biases from interfering with my journey of discovery.

One of the best things you can do to mitigate the effects of blind spots in your life is to challenge your beliefs. I followed a pattern of asking.

"What do I believe is true?"
"Why do I believe it is true?"

"Can I be absolutely certain it is true?"

"What if is not true?"

"How would I feel if it was not true?"

"Am I willing to change my belief if the evidence points to a different reality?"

Living at the speed of modern life, I never sat down long enough to ask these questions. I never really challenged my own beliefs. I started this process from a spiritual vantage point, and what I learned was startling. My quest revealed that I held contradictory beliefs. Since the purpose of this book is not religious in nature, I will refrain from sharing the questions and answers. But what I discovered was that I'd held beliefs learned from listening to preachers over many years, and some of the lessons from these preachers contradicted one another. Yet I didn't realize this until I started questioning! Since these contradictions existed, I needed to study the source of the beliefs, the Bible, in a way I'd never done before.

I approached studying the ancient text with a very unemotional, rational, structured pursuit. I learned a methodology called Hermeneutics. That is a scientific approach to studying ancient manuscripts. How this works, and what I discovered, revealed the errors of my various beliefs and changed the disposition of my Christianity. I continue to choose the Christian faith in Jesus Christ, but I approach faith with much more skepticism than ever before. As author William Lane Craig states in the title of his book, I believe I now have a more "reasonable faith." If you would like more information about my spiritual pursuits and how I learned to study the Bible along with the resources I used, please visit:

www.UltimateBlindSpot.com

These challenge questions hold true for non-spiritual beliefs as well. Think, for instance, about a news report. Whether you watch and listen to a news report on a liberal or conservative station, you will be hearing a very biased version of the facts. Imagine running those reports through this filter:

"Is this news report true?"
"Can I be absolutely certain it's true?"
"What if it not true?"

If you have a liberal bias, you are easily susceptible to confirmation bias and might think what you are hearing *must* be true. The same holds true for the conservative camps. You unconsciously look for information to support the values and beliefs you hold. The longer you've held those beliefs, the more indoctrinated they are in your life, and the harder they are to change. In fact, you don't even consider change unless a major event takes place, something that shakes up your entire world. I don't really recommend prison, but it did work out for me.

Whether conservative or liberal, does the media you read, watch or listen to fuel your position? Are you actively seeking the opposing perspectives and weighing the evidence yourself?

Maybe it's time to start challenging why you believe what you believe.

RDAP APPROVED

I was fortunate to become eligible for a program in the prison called RDAP – Residential Drug Alcohol Program. It is a 500-classroom-hour, nine-month in-residence training program based on CBT, or Cognitive Behavioral Therapy psychology. Most of the participants have a serious drug or alcohol problem, but the only technical qualification is *any* level of drinking or drug use. Since I enjoy an occasional adult beverage, especially one with a little umbrella while sitting in the hot sun on a white beach, I was qualified and accepted. Okay, I live in

Oregon, so there's not so much hot sun. Come on, a guy has to have a dream, right?

What I learned in this program further helped me figure out how I had been duped, and how I could make better decisions in the future. The program and learning also fueled my passion to help others make better decisions. After better understanding how the mind works, I discovered a simple formula about our thinking process, and how it is affected by our worldview and decisions.

SYSTEM 1 AND SYSTEM 2

When you witness an event or stimuli, you perceive the event and instantly filter that perception through the framework of your worldview. This usually happens unconsciously. Daniel Kahneman in his book, *Thinking, Fast and Slow*, calls this "System 1." This is your unconscious thinking system that allows you to function without having to constantly think about what you are doing.

For instance, once you have learned to drive and practiced long enough, you no longer consciously think about how to make a right turn. When you want to turn right, you do so. You don't have to think, "Okay, I need to turn the steering wheel to the right and continue turning it until I am moving the vehicle in the correct direction."

System 1 allows you to simply make the turn without a single conscious thought. System 1 is intuitive, fast and emotional. System 1 is constantly learning and processing stimuli by way of association. It continuously helps you make sense of reality as it frames your worldview.

It is System 1 that is constantly creating and depending on 'heuristics' – basically, guidelines and general rules. System 1 is where impressions are formed and fed to System 2. These impressions help you in times of danger, but can be less accurate in other times.

System 2 is more deliberate; it's slow and logical. It is your conscious, rational thinking, which can override the impressions from System 1. However, it is often oblivious to the fact that it is being misled by System 1, so there's no chance for an override. Hence, blind spots!

This is the point at which you need to deliberately engage System 2 and challenge what is happening in System 1. System 1 perceives the event or stimuli and filters it through the framework of your worldview. System 1 then generates impressions, unconscious or sometimes conscious thoughts and feelings. From those feelings you will typically act, react or not act at all. A simplistic view of this process is:

Event (or Stimuli) – Perception – Thought – Feeling – Behavior.

S-T-P FORMULA

To change your behavior, you can interrupt the pattern and challenge System 1 using the S-T-P formula. That is, when you experience a thought or feeling, you can challenge it, in order to create a more desirable decision and outcome. You engage your rational thinking, System 2, by employing S-T-P: Stop – Think – Process (then Proceed).

In other words, when you have a thought, feeling or impression that is inappropriate or undesirable, you need to immediately take command of your thinking and stop to challenge it. You might ask, "What did I just experience or perceive? Is that perception true? Can I be sure it is true? Is what I'm thinking and/or feeling leading to a desirable outcome?"

To challenge your thoughts and feelings, simply ask questions appropriate to the situation. For instance, as Malcolm Gladwell describes in *Blink*, when a police officer sees what is thought to be a gun, they are highly trained to immediately react and place themselves in positions of safety. They're also trained to place a distance of time between the actual event, and their reaction to the event. By doing so, they are able activate System 2 and rationally evaluate what they really saw. What is the true level of danger? Did they see a gun? Could the person be reaching for a wallet instead? System 1 is protecting the officer. System 2 is potentially protecting the other party.

The new formula for challenging your thinking and replacing the *initial* thought with a *new* thought looks like this:

Event (or Stimuli) – Perception – Thought – Feeling – STP – New Thought – New Feeling – More Desirable Behavior.

In other words, the event takes place. You perceive the event, and System 1 processes it in an instant. A thought, feeling or impression is generated. You stop before you react so that you can think about what you are perceiving and feeling. You then rationally replace or affirm the initial thought and act accordingly.

Have you ever been walking down the hallway at work and happened to catch a glimpse of someone who appears to be looking at you funny? For some reason as your eyes meet, the expression on their face is disturbing to you. You get this sense or feeling that they have an issue with you, even though you've done nothing wrong. You might even think to yourself, irritated, "What is that look all about? What's up buddy?!"

At this moment, you have a choice.

You could just let System 1 interpret the event, and act or react according to that interpretation. Or, you could S-T-P and change your thought. Say you choose the latter. You catch yourself feeling offended. So, you stop yourself from reacting. You think, "Hmm. I wonder what that look was about. Maybe it has nothing to do with me. Maybe they didn't even see me; maybe they were looking right through me." You decide to discard the entire event and move on – to not act at all. Maybe you create a new thought that prompts you to stop and compassionately ask if everything is okay.

In either case, you avoided a potential conflict by not reacting to your interpretation of the look on someone's face. What if they actually *did* have an issue with you, you ask? Well, your first choice in this scenario would be to simply avoid conflict and move on. Maybe they'll get over whatever was on their mind. If not, there will be another opportunity to resolve the situation. Your second option would likely reveal the situation. But, because you took a compassionate, non-combative approach, you reduced the likelihood of escalating the conflict.

The S-T-P Formula is a powerful heuristic to reduce internal and external conflict. Try it!

COUNTDOWN TO THE DOOR

As a guy approached the end of his sentence, we called it the "Countdown to the Door." Once we hit the ninety-nine-day mark, we became *double-digit midgets*. I realize the phrase does not sound politically correct, but, well, it was a prison. It wasn't addressed to any particular group; it was just the phrase used for those of us who had fewer than one hundred days before we were released.

For some, this became a horrifying experience. A guy might be thinking he's getting out, and the next thing he knows he's being detained. Imagine the *single*-digit midget who is counting down his final nine days to get out of prison early as a result of good behavior, when suddenly he's told he's not going anywhere. It's as if the guards walk him to the door, quickly close it, then turn and say, "Psyche! Haha, gotcha! You're not going anywhere, pal!"

It's profoundly disappointing and discouraging. The worst is, it could have been avoided. Most of the time, the delays are due to some state agency simply not closing out a pending case before it was transferred to the feds. Just prior to release, the feds check the national criminal databases. When they see a pending case they are required to detain the inmate.

When this happens, it is devastating to the guy who was ready to get on with rebuilding his life. The longer the original sentence, the worse the devastation. For an inmate serving a five-year sentence, for instance, he would normally be released about nine months early if he maintained good behavior. But, if he gets detained at the last minute, he could spend as much as nine months more in prison – all because of a clerical error.

I didn't know anyone personally who experienced this detainer process, but some of the guys did. For most of us, being a double-digit midget was the most exciting time.

Every day was a countdown. I could hardly wait to get home to Rachel, Chris and Noelle. Rachel was excited for me to come home, but she was also a bit anxious that I would upset their new way of life. I assured her to continue business as usual; Joe had wisely advised me to not expect to walk back in to the house as the leader. He suggested that I just flow with however life was happening at home. It was excellent advice, and it worked out for everyone. In our household, prior to going to prison, I was given the mantle of leadership. But afterwards, I couldn't go back to the house and just start wielding my position; I had to earn their respect.

Action Tip: Earn the respect of your significant other and your children, and life will go well with you.

Positional versus earned leadership is not just a principle for the workplace.

Over the last year or so, in tandem with personal growth studies and launching back into a speaking career, I was also revising the business plan for Ron's dental financing business. I'd earned his trust during the two years leading up to sentencing, and now he wanted me to resume my role as President of that business unit.

When I left, the manager of the business unit tried to keep it running in my absence, but he was able to barely keep it afloat. So, expecting me to step back in and grow the company, Ron mailed me any information and market research I requested. I used the data to create a business plan and financial forecast in preparation for my return. I realize that I was incredibly blessed to have his trust, to have a job waiting for me upon release. Not many guys had the same opportunities, and getting out could sometimes be just as hard as getting in.

Even though the company was based in Seattle, Ron agreed to open a satellite office in whichever city I resided. This was especially helpful, as Rachel had moved her and the family from Washington to Oregon to be closer for our visits. I was released on May 1, 2007, but part of the integration process was to go directly to a halfway house before going home.

DRUG ADDICTS, PIMPS AND PROSTITUTES

I was released to the Lane County Jail Annex, a halfway house connected to the county jail. The Federal Bureau of Prisons rented space in the annex, populated by local drug addicts, thieves, and prostitutes. The annex, a smaller secure living quarters with rooms and cots instead of cells, was primarily used as a place of transition for inmates getting out of jail and entering back in to society. According to one of the staff members, the jail that fed the annex had an eighty-eight percent recidivism rate. Eighty-eight percent! Think of any cop show on television that shows the craziness of their local jail and you will have a good idea of what this place was like. It was the complete opposite of the federal prison camp.

The only saving grace was that there were seven federal inmates who all shared a single room with seven cots. It was the 'fed room,' and we all hung out together for meals, or just in the dorm. The federal inmates had several privileges not afforded to the normal clientele. We had the right to leave the halfway house for church services; we could also join a local health club and work out every day if we wanted. If we didn't want to join the club, we could simply walk around the block on a predefined route.

Michael and I did all of these things as often as we were allowed. Michael was a new friend I met in the annex, a federal inmate who was transferred to Oregon from New Jersey. He was an enforcer for an East coast crime family, and nothing intimidated him. In his youth, he had been a person of faith, but strayed off the path in his line of work. His journey took him down some very scary roads. During his eight-year prison sentence, however, he reached back out to his faith and turned his life around. That's when we got to know each other; we enjoyed hanging out and attending church together.

We also hung out with another older gentleman named Andre. He was only fifty-three years old, but looked like he was in his seventies. He was from Georgia, and had requested a transfer to get as far from his old life as possible. Andre had robbed more than thirty banks in his career. He spent more days of his life in prison than he did out of prison, and he wanted desperately to retire his life of crime.

Andre secured a job as a dishwasher of a local restaurant, just blocks from the halfway house. The owners felt bad for him, and gave him a cot in the basement where he could live.

One day, after we were released, Michael and I realized we hadn't heard from Andre in while. When we inquired, we discovered he'd robbed another bank and got caught. He told the business owner that he just couldn't handle life on the outside.

He had been institutionalized. Prison was all he knew. Robbing another bank and purposely getting caught would send him back to the life he understood.

Michael and I eventually went our separate ways. I'm not sure where he is today, but I heard he was struggling.

My heart goes out to those who struggle to break free from their old lives, their old ways of thinking. Maybe you're not struggling with a life of crime; maybe you struggle with addiction. Maybe your struggles are the war that rages in your mind as you try to fight limiting beliefs. Whatever you struggle with, S-T-P can help. Challenge your beliefs. Challenge the thinking that holds you back. Challenge what you currently believe about yourself. You don't have to remain the same. You can change. You can become the person you desire to be!

> *Blind Spot Challenge: What triggers cause you to react in undesirable ways? Use S-T-P.*

You *are* who you *think* you are. When you change your thinking, you will change your life. If you can't get a breakthrough on you own, seek help from a friend, pastor, loved one, or professional counselor. Do whatever it takes to create a new mindset. Changing your behavior starts with changing your thinking.

A friend once asked me, "What was the biggest lesson you learned in prison?" I said, "Blind spots. We all have them." That statement birthed what has become a successful new brand called *The BlindSpot Zone*™.

CHAPTER NINE:

WHERE DO WE GO FROM HERE?

PIVOT

"'Pivoting' is a familiar word in the startup world. When your first business model isn't working (and this happens more often than not), the CEO and team pivot to Plan B. These are deep-breath moments!

But pivoting doesn't necessarily mean desperation. It can be a tool to discover additional growth – growth you might have overlooked."[40]

In the same way, as individuals we sometimes need to pivot. Maybe you have been displaced at work and find yourself wondering what to do next. Maybe you're simply burned out and need a change. Maybe an accident has altered your mental or physical abilities to continue your current profession.

Or, maybe you have a criminal record and now struggle to find a new path?

The list can go on ad infinitum. There will always be *pivot* moments. Life happens. Sometimes you get knocked down without warning. Sometimes you are forced to deal with change, and it's not comfortable. The real question becomes: *how are you going to handle it?* In these moments, you can either get bitter, or you can choose to get better. Embrace the change; look for a new perspective that will help you adapt with a great attitude. Don't let the current framework of your

---

[40] Spoon, Alan (2012, Aug 10). *What 'Pivot' really means*. Retrieved from https://www.inc.com/alan-spoon/what-pivot-really-means.html. Emphasis added.

reality become blind spots; don't let them keep you from seeing new perspectives, or opening up to new possibilities.

Since being released from prison I've had to pivot several times. I couldn't share this story at first, and believe me, I tried. While working for the dental patient financing business, I found a few opportunities to share this story with audiences locally. But after my fourth speech, I had to quit! I realized I was not emotionally ready to share. I didn't understand how to frame up the lessons in a meaningful way. The scars had not yet healed. My self-esteem was in the toilet. So, I put that dream on hold.

Then the 2008 recession hit. We had to close down the dental patient financing business, because too many patients were defaulting. Ron continued to pay off all current clients, but he stopped taking on new ones.

Thankfully, through a connection with Rachel's longtime college friend, I was offered a job with a startup software company as their trainer. When we discovered the software was not ready to take to market, I became their chief technology officer for a season. Once the software was ready for deployment, in addition to managing the programming and support teams, I also trained end-users and salespeople.

While continuing to work for the software company, I joined the National Speakers Association (NSA) Oregon chapter in 2009 as a candidate. I started looking for speaking opportunities part-time, on top of my corporate work, and was accepted as a professional member at the national level in 2013. Then, in 2014, I resigned from the software company and started speaking full time for the first time since the 1990's – and I haven't looked back! NSA Oregon voted me Chapter Member of the Year in 2015, and I became President of the Chapter for 2017-18.

Rachel and I celebrated our thirtieth wedding anniversary in August 2016, and look forward to celebrating many more. Chris is a creative director and manages the website design division of a larger firm, and Noelle, now married to her college sweetheart, Jaron, graduated college with honors. She is currently a top producing recruiter for an employment firm, and her husband is finishing his higher education degrees while working as a professor of philosophy. We're incredibly proud of all three of them.

There is an old saying that when life throws you lemons, make lemonade. I have a different version: when your blind spots land you in prison, *make microwave cheesecakes*!

CONCLUSION

During my keynote speeches, I typically provide time to answer questions. In almost every instance the audience wants to know the same thing: *what happened to Lawrence?* Facing 25-30 years if he lost in a trial, and he undoubtedly would have, he eventually signed a 20-year plea bargain. He is still in prison with an expected release date of January 3, 2020 at which time he will have served just over 16 years of his sentence. Ten other men, seven of which, I believe, were also unwitting accomplices, received sentences ranging from 6 months to 12 ½ years. Jackson, the former stock broker, received a 7-year sentence. Wes, who originally sold me the stock, was never charged. How Wes, Craig and several others avoided criminal charges remains a mystery.

Blind spots affect all of us in our personal and professional lives. They affect your relationships at work and home. Blind spots affect you in leadership, hiring, sales, auditing, investigations, customer service and overall productivity. They hit you hard in your financial life. We sometimes become victims of fraud or other financial crimes because of our own blind spots. Blind spots reduce the effectiveness of your work groups and teams, and hinder organizations from creating diverse and inclusive cultures. Blind spots empower the voices in our heads that tell us we're not good enough. They create the artificial barriers that hinder us from living happy, joyful, peaceful lives. In other words, blind spots affect us all at times in many different areas of life – so it's essential to become more aware of these blind spots and learn to use tools to mitigate them.

To help you apply these principles and move *Beyond the Blind-Spot Zone*™, download a complimentary copy of the *BlindSpot Zone Information System* at:

www.KevinMcCarthy.com/ZONE

For bulk orders of this book or to inquire about speaking availability for your next conference or corporate event, church service, men's group or retreat, contact me directly.

One of the most sought-after programs is a fun, dynamic and content-rich parody called:

THE BLINDSPOT ZONE™

DISCOVER YOUR LEADERSHIP BLIND SPOTS!

GET YOUR FREE ASSESSMENT

Available at

www.KevinMcCarthy.com/BSA

Kevin McCarthy
+1-877-527-9613
+1-503-427-8531

Connect with the author at:

Website: www.KevinMcCarthy.com

LinkedIn: www.LinkedIn.com/in/SpeakerKevinMcCarthy

Twitter: www.Twitter.com/KevinMcCarthy01

www.KevinMcCarthy.com/FreeKindleOffer

Index of Blind Spots

Index of Blind Spot Challenges

Index of Action Tips